Managing the Nursing priorities in intensive care

We dedicate this book to both of our families for the support, encouragement, patience and love that they have each given in their different ways

Other titles in the Key Management Skills in Nursing Series

Dementia
  by I B McIntosh and K Woodall
Management in the Acute Ward
  by J Walton and M Reeves
Managing the Ethical Process in Research
  by M Hammick
Managing Continuing Education
  by M Williams
Learning Skills, Studying Styles and Profiling
  by R A Brown and B Hawksley
Promoting Health: An Issue for Nursing
  by N Mackintosh
Deep Vein Thrombosis: The Silent Killer
  by R Autar
Nursing Expertise and Advanced Practice
  by J Conway
Learning Journals and Critical Incidents
  by S Lillyman and T Ghaye
Managing Pressure Sore Prevention
  by C Dealey

**Key Management Skills in Nursing
Series**
Editor: R A Brown

Managing the nursing priorities in intensive care

John W Albarran and Theresa E Price

Quay
Books

Quay Books Division, Mark Allen Publishing Group,
Jesses Farm, Snow Hill, Dinton, Nr Salisbury, Dinton,
Wiltshire, SP3 5HN

© Mark Allen Publishing Group Ltd, 1998

British Library Cataloguing-in-Publication Data
A catalogue record for this book is available from the British
Library

ISBN 1 85642 038 8

Printed in the UK by Redwood Books, Trowbridge, Wiltshire

Contents

Acknowledgements

We would like to thank L Miller from the ITU in Frenchay Hospital, Bristol and J Crampton from the ITU at Southmead Hospital, Bristol, for their constructive comments, suggestions and advice.

We would also like to acknowledge Lesley Donovan, Head of Adult School, Faculty of Health and Social Care, University of the West of England, Bristol, for her continued support and understanding in the completion of this project.

Introduction

The premise of this text is that the effective management of patient care begins with the accurate assessment and interpretation of patient data, in order that the nursing plan of interventions reflects the uniqueness of a patients' priorities as well as the distinctiveness of the nurses' contribution to the delivery of holistic care.

In this book, each section has been organised around the following headings with the purpose of producing a coherent and accessible resource:

- objectives of the chapter, aetiology and definition of terms
- assessment of priorities for nursing care and patient problems
- managing the priorities of a patient's care (including medical interventions and nursing strategies)
- associated complications
- reference list.

While the titles of each chapter suggest a physiological focus, it will become apparent that, as appropriate, each section addresses a range of areas including, patient assessment, contemporary nursing strategies for care and innovations in clinical practice. Moreover, throughout each chapter there has been a stress on the nursing perspective as well as on identifying the core skills that are necessary for organising the delivery of high quality care to a range of clinical conditions.

Intensive care is both demanding and challenging, arguably this also applies to identifying and meeting the priorities of patient care. The view submitted here, is that the effectiveness of a nurse has to be underpinned by a set of competencies which should consist of being able to conduct a comprehensive assessment, thus allowing for the selection of relevant data to guide decision-making. Combined with these attributes, should be the skills of being able to discern the subtlety of a situation as well as the significance of clinical changes and demonstrating advanced competence in supplying accurate diagnoses. Finally, the ability to institute appropriate interventions which encompass evidence-based practice are aspects that not only enhance the patient's health but illustrate how nurses make a difference to patient outcomes. It is intended that the particular structure adopted in this project will emphasise these fundamental beliefs and that advancing patient care relies on a combination of elements where the utilisation of research findings is a central component.

With regard to the nursing priorities, several themes have emerged in writing this book. Priorities of care are never static, while some basic principles may remain constant, the process of managing care is continuously evolving and in the sense these are dynamic. A secondary issue is that many clinical priorities of care are not always discipline-led, many are interchangeable and, indeed, this is appropriate. Although how each profession achieves this may be distinct. Thirdly, the priorities in this text have been deliberately based on a nursing perspective with the purpose of guiding the reader and for structuring our ideas. This is not to imply that patients or others in this field may concur with this or rank them in a similar order of importance. Finally, deciding where the pre-eminence of care lies seems context-dependent as this shifts according to the patient's needs, the assessment of clinical status and whether the priorities have been communicated. However, there is a definite recognition that artistry in intensive care nursing is also about organisation and management which results from seeing the objectives of patient care in short, medium and long term goals.

In conclusion, it is hoped that the approach taken in this textbook provides a particular style, that is discursive, thought provoking, informed and captures the spirit of the core skills demanded of intensive care nurses. It has been equally stressed that to justify professional accountability for patient care, nursing interventions must be dominated by the implementation of relevant research findings. Moreover, the integration of evidence-based practice can be viewed not only as a means of promoting the quality of patient outcomes, but also that the philosophy provides nurses with the opportunity to demonstrate the impact of the profession on national health service targets (Cook *et al*, 1996; Kitson, 1997). Inevitably, while the intelligent prioritising of care is one step towards successful patient outcomes, acquiring skills in assessing, interpreting, diagnosing and evaluating is also critical to this endeavour, as must be the ability to transfer this repertoire to a spectrum of clinical situations.

John W Albarran, June 1997

References

Cook DJ, Sibbald W, Vincent JL *et al* (1996) Evidence-based critical care medicine: what is it and what can it do for us? *Critical Care Medicine* **24**(2): 334–337

Kitson A, (1997) Using evidence to demonstrate the value of nursing. *Nurs Stand* **11**(28): 34–39

1

Managing the nursing priorities in the mechanically ventilated patient

Introduction

The aim of this chapter is to discuss the priorities of care for patients who require artificial ventilation.

Objectives of this chapter:

- to analyse and identify the priorities of nursing care for patients who require mechanical ventilation (MV)
- to discuss current nursing care strategies for this group of patients
- to identify the complications associated with mechanical ventilation.

West (1990) suggests that patients with respiratory failure are those who need artificial respiratory support. Characteristically, respiratory failure is defined when the lungs fail to adequately oxygenate the arterial blood or fail to prevent the retention of carbon dioxide. Typically, the patient may have an arterial oxygen (PO_2) of less than 80mmHg (or 7.5Kpa, normal 12–15Kpa) despite oxygen therapy and or an arterial carbon dioxide (PCO_2) of greater 40mmHg or 6Kpa (normal 4–6Kpa) to meet the criteria of hypoxaemia.

Causes of acute respiratory failure and identification of patient problems

Classifications of respiratory failure in the adult patient can be extensive, however the main causes of hypoxaemia can be divided into four key areas:

1) Primary lung pathology

This refers to the destructive lung processes where there is loss of lung function. This can include *loss of compliance* due to tissue scarring or lung fibrosis. In contrast, an increase in dead space (*Figure 1.2*) refers to a situation in which the alveoli may be ventilated but due to poor blood supply they are not well perfused, thus, there is ventilation in excess of perfusion. This is referred to as an V/Q (ventilation/ perfusion) mismatch (West, 1990). A common cause of this is a pulmonary embolous, where a blocked vessel may affect the blood supply to a number of alveoli and so ventilation in these areas is *wasted*. Although in the unaffected lung units gas exchange will remain unchanged. Other causes include vasospasm and disseminated intravascular coagulation. In a respiratory shunt, (*Figure 1.3*) however, blood may enter and leave the pulmonary system without receiving oxygen, this is because although the circulation is intact the alveoli are underventilated either due to collapse, consolidation or mucus congestion. Here there is also an alteration in V/Q ratio in that perfusion exceeds ventilation and due to problems with diffusion, gas exchange is impaired. In health it is the distribution of blood flow (cardiac output) and ventilation (tidal volume) across lung regions which plays a key role in the maintenance of arterial oxygenation (*Figure 1.1*) (West, 1990). Among the lung diseases found in this group are pneumonia, chronic obstructive pulmonary disease, asthma, atelectasis, direct lung trauma, and Adult Respiratory Distress Syndrome (ARDS).

Figure 1.1: Normal ventilation and perfusion

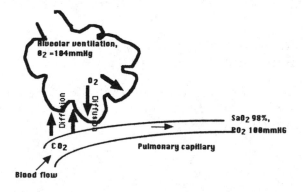

Figure 1.2: Ventilation in excess of perfusion (increase in alveolar dead space)

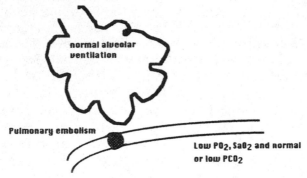

Figure 1.3: Perfusion in excess of ventilation (pulmonary shunt)

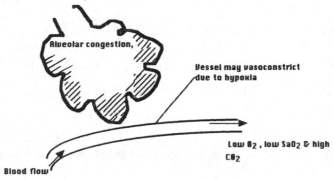

2) Disruption to neuromuscular control of ventilation

In health respiration is controlled by the brain stem relaying messages along the spinal cord to the intercostal and abdominal muscles, diaphragm and other accessory muscles. It follows that any damage to this network will compromise the maintenance of respiration.

• Central causes: Head injuries are one group, where a rise in intracranial pressure due to either a space occupying lesion or cerebral oedema will disrupt the control of respiration by increasing pressure on the brain stem. These changes are also likely to occur with cerebrovascular accidents. In contrast, over-dosage of narcotics, barbiturates and benzodiazepines depress the respiratory centre and suppress the cough reflex. This can have serious consequences for the patient as the risk of aspiration is increased. Infections such as meningitis can also be included under this heading, as the associated loss of consciousness and inflamatory neurological changes can compromise respiratory functioning (Stillwell, 1996)

- Injury to the spinal cord: If an injury to the spinal cord is at a high cervical level, it can result in permanent paralysis of all the muscles of respiration. Trauma and diving in shallow water can lead to transection of the spinal cord. In tetanus, the nerve cells of the spinal cord are affected resulting in spasms of skeletal muscles although if the respiratory motor neurones are involved respiratory distress ensues

- Diseases of the peripheral nerves:The most common disease in this category is Guillan-Barre syndrome in which the patient presents with progressive weakness that can involve loss of respiratory and swallowing functions. It is usually preceded by a flu-like illness.

3) Pathology of other organs/systems affecting lung functioning

- A prolonged cardiac arrest has the potential to cause a V/Q disturbance which may result in hypoxaemia. In constrast pulmonary oedema can lead to hypoxia (*Figure 1.3*)

- A pulmonary embolus can result in an increase in dead space, inhibit the loss of PCO_2 and, due to the reduction in lung compliance, promote arterial hypoxemia (*Figure 1.2*).

4) Disruption to the anatomical mechanics of ventilation

- A chest wall injury: This is where the typical 'flail' chest movements are apparent. As a result of damage to a segment of the chest wall, the affected side moves inwards during inspiration and pushed outwards in expiration, the reverse of normal respiration

- Haemothorax and pneumothorax: This is when there is either blood, air or fluid within the chest cavity preventing the lung from expanding naturally. One of the most serious conditions is a tension pneumothorax. Air can be trapped in the pleural space without means of escape, the patient may rapidly become breathless and dyspnoeic. The affected lung may collapse and due to the increase in compression, the heart and major vessels may shift to one side which in turn reduces the patient's cardiac output

- Post-surgical: Many operations may be complex and prolonged, some patients may have accumulated high levels of anaesthetic agents and thus it may not be possible to extubate them without compromising their safety. Pain and limited chest mobility are typical after cardiac surgery, this may interfere with lung and diaphragmatic expansion. In addition, patients may have received intravenous sedation during this period thus a short period of MV may be advantageous

- Conditions affecting the trachea, larynx and epiglottis due to an infection or inflammatory response can obstruct the airway and place the patient's airway at risk.

In these situations the patient may require a period of MV, this can be by means of a nasal or oral endotracheal tube (ETT) or by way of a tracheostomy, although the medical management will be shaped to a large extent by the underlying aetiology. Similarly, the individual with acute respiratory failure or who is unconscious will present the nurse with a unique set of patient problems which demand assessment. These will centre around airway maintenance, the retention of sputum, insufficient oxygenation, altered respiratory pattern and cognitive state. For example, a loss of lung compliance, pulmonary shunting, or an increase in dead space will inhibit the diffusion of gases. Whereas the lack of adequate breathing and hypoventilation will also alter the patient's acid-base balance thus worsening the neurological state and overall condition of the individual.

From a nursing perspective the primary objectives must thus be to secure and protect the patient's airway, to optimise respiratory functioning, to promote comfort and an early uncomplicated recovery. However, to achieve this, other areas of care must be equally managed. For example, all patients should have their pain under control, their skin integrity and personal hygiene maintained, nutritional and elimination needs met, be protected against infections and their families supported (Ashurst, 1997a; Stillwell, 1996). Of equal importance with this client group is the need for communication, whether verbal or non-verbal, for restoring identity, developing a therapeutic relationship, giving confidence, maintaining sensory balance, providing emotional stability and support, and so minimising confusional states (Albarran, 1991; Dyer, 1995a, b; Pearce, 1994). Cutcliffe (1996) also discusses how for a patient, a sense of hope can add to their coping resources and confidence, as well as being an aspect which is interwoven with therapeutic caring. While these elements may be regarded as core basic clinical skills they remain at the heart of effective nursing practice as they form the basis for developing the more complex and technical skills.

Assessing the priorities for nursing care

To identify and effectively manage the priorities of care in a patient needing MV, requires that the nurse conducts a systematic assessment of physical and psychosocial needs in order that the strategy of care reflects the immediate and long term goals.

The assessment should include:

- a review of the patient's history — reasons for admission, known medical background (COAD, asthma, chest trauma, aspiration of gastric contents), is the patient a smoker, what medications are taken at home, other relevant history, temperature, blood pressure and heart rate patterns
- ventilatory review — it is essential that this should include the size of ETT, mode of ventilation, preset respiratory values and the means of humidifying the airway; assessing for evidence of pulmonary sounds on auscultation and for equal chest movements is important, as is an examination of the colour and texture of sputum. Radiological appraisal, and whether the patient is able to work with a physiotherapist also play a role in decision-making
- gas exchange analysis — this involves determining the severity of hypoxaemia or metabolic derangement, the response to initial treatment (supplemental

oxygenation, or endotracheal intubation and MV) or
the effects of specific ventilatory measures (PEEP,
and bronchodilators) on the patient. In addition the
on-going interpretation of trends may be guided by
pulse oximetry reading

- supportive nursing measures should encompass what
  is being provided in terms of pain relief, what is the
  state of sedation level required, does the patient need
  hydration, is a naso-gastric tube in place, how soon
  can nutrition commence? Obtaining a background on
  the patient's family and close relationships is also a
  requisite in organising supportive care for the
  individual during acute and recovery phases. Central
  to the assessment of these patients must be
  identifying the appropriate means for communication
  and information sharing.

For nurses to improve the patient's condition and well being,
their knowledge, experience and skills must be applied to
analysing, interpreting, evaluating data and for
discriminating the subtleties that are embedded within the
complex care environment. However, to manage the priorities
of nursing care, (*Table 1.1*) this must be in combination with
the prescribed medical treatment and complimentary to the
contributions of other health care staff.

Management of the patient's care

Overall, the principle elements of treatment in a large
number of mechanically ventilated patients are similar,
however the underlying condition will dictate the need for
specific nursing or medical interventions. This may include
bronchodilators, antibiotics, plasmapharesis, skeletal
traction and modified ventilation manoeuvres.

Table 1.1: Priorities of care for a mechanically ventilated patient

Nursing priorities	Intervention/management
Airway maintenance and safety	• providing humidification • endotracheal suctioning • securing ETT in place
Promoting oxygenation	• delivery of oxygen therapy • positive end expiratory pressure • use of patient posture
Monitoring respiratory progress and comfort	• ventilatory parameters maintained • arterial blood gases • sedation level • complications of MV
Safe and uncomplicated weaning of MV	• optimising clinical status • providing physical and emotional support

Airway maintenance and safety

Ashurst (1997a) suggests that because oral cuffed tubes are easier to insert they are more commonly employed but, as they are very mobile and difficult to hold in place, they may cause problems with oral and laryngeal irritation, lip trauma, hypersalivation, pain and discomfort. In contrast, a nasal tube is much more stable as it is held secure in the nasal cavity. This helps to maintain oral functioning, reduces the incidence of gagging and is well tolerated by patients. But, due to the added length, a nasal airway increases the dead space and as such ETT suctioning becomes more difficult. There is also a risk of sinusitis if a nasal tube is left in place for a length of time.

A patient who has an ETT in place will lose the natural resources provided within the nasal and the upper airways, including humidifying, filtering and warming of inspired gases. These protective mechanisms prevent damage to the tracheal tree caused by the inhalation of dry gases but also inhibit impairment of the mucociliary elevator and alterations in the viscosity of chest secretions (Ballard *et al*, 1992; Jackson, 1996).

The consequences of a lack of humidification within respiratory airways can threaten the patient who is intubated as there is a risk of secretions becoming dry and viscous which in turn may lead to actelectasis and either narrowing or blocking of the airway. Additionally, any damage to the cilia, epithelial structures and other mucosal membranes will hinder the transfer of heat and moisture to inspired gas and thus contribute to the dryness of mucus. Therefore, when patients are intubated it is vital that inspired gases are warmed and humidified.

Currently there are various means by which humidification can be provided in a ventilatory circuit, this can be either by a heat and moisture exchange (HME) device, heated wire water bath humidifiers. HMEs work on the basis that they preserve the heat and moisture produced during expiration and return this to the patient on the following breath, thus closely reproducing the functions of the upper airways (Joynt and Lipman, 1994). Although there are derivations on this, they all seek to provide optimal humidification and moisturising of gases, although some incorporate a microbiological filtering function. This characteristic helps to prevent the contamination of infected sputum from patients to staff as well as to expensive ventilator equipment, thereby reducing the frequency of ventilator circuit changes (Branson and Chatburn, 1993; Joynt and Lipman, 1994). Arguably, their small size, simplicity of use and reduced risk of cross infection helps to explain their wide usage.

While very few complications relate to the use of an HME, it is advocated that for patients with thickened and tenacious sputum, a water bath humidification system should be used, as well as for those with hypothermia of less than 32°C (Branson and Chatburn, 1993; Joynt and Lipman, 1994). Caution is also required with some nebulised bronchial medications as the efficency of an HME can be impaired.

Unlike HMEs, heated humidifiers rely on a heating element and water bath which is able to deliver water vapour above the room temperature, thereby increasing the warmth and moisture of inspired gas (Ballard *et al*, 1992). They are unlikely to produce or prolong the length of hypothermia and shivering which has been reported in ventilated ITU patients and those recovering after cardiac surgery, which has been observed with the use of HMEs alone (Martin *et al*, 1990; McEvoy and Carey, 1995). However, many of the problems associated with heated baths stem from the risks of bacterial contamination of the ventilator circuit, the level of condensation produced which may cause resistance to gas flow, variations in efficiency of the humidity, costs of maintenance, electrical hazards and the risks of thermal injury (Ballard *et al*, 1992). Jackson (1996) also adds that the risks of overheating the inspired gas can lead to hyperthermia and that an increase in humidification can add to pulmonary congestion. Although the use of humidifiers with a heating wire within the inspiratory and expiratory arms of the ventilator circuit can reduce the level of condensation they may also increase the absolute humidity. This, in turn, can adversely promote consolidation of airway secretions by changing the degree of relative humidity within the ventilator tubing (Miyao *et al*, 1996).

In considering the choice of humidifier, nurses must evaluate the patients pulmonary secretions and temperature before a decision is made about means of respiratory humification. More recently in a randomised study of 200 patients, it was reported that in surgical patients an HME was adequate for their humification needs (Branson *et al*, 1996). However, those with underlying respiratory disease, tended to have thicker and greater volumes of pulmonary secretions and, as such, needed to be managed with heated humidification, as well as requiring longer periods of MV than their general surgical counterparts. Because of the need to clear water condensation which collects in the ventilatory circuit, those patients treated with a water bath were more at risk of infection due to higher disconnection rates, thereby adding to the overall costs of care. On the basis of their findings, Branson *et al* (1996) developed an algorithm to guide nurses in determining the appropriate means for humidification that is linked to the individual needs of the patient.

For many critically ill patients the ability to clear secretions is compromised because the ETT bypasses a large part of the upper airways. This will affect the retention of mucus and the situation will be worsened in the presence of respiratory disease, chest trauma, supressed or absent cough reflex, thoracic surgery and unconsciousness. To prevent the accumulation of sputum, lung collapse and to maintain the patency of the patients' airway, periodic suctioning in combination with physiotherapy and humidification are the key functions.

Passing a suction catheter into an endotracheal/ tracheostomy tube is not without risks, for example dysrhythmias, hypoxia, and trauma. It is thus important that a nurse assesses the relevant patient indicators prior to the procedure (Fiorentini, 1992). These may include a sudden rise in inspiratory pressure, audible secretions during respiration, reduced breath sounds, colour and tenacity of sputum, evidence of crepitations on asculation (Odell *et al*, 1993). The colour of the patient, coughing spasms, limited chest movements, alterations in blood gases and a drop in oxygen saturation are other essential criteria which indicate a need for immediate suctioning.

The use of intermittent negative suction pressure of between 15–20Kpa is currently recommended, as a higher negative pressure can lead to mucosal damage and scarring (Odell *et al*, 1993). Prior to suctioning the nurse must ascertain the size of the airway before selecting a catheter, in practice this should be half the internal diameter of the endotracheal tube and the manoeuvre should last no longer than fifteen seconds (Ashurst, 1992; Hooper, 1996). Based on a critical review of the research, Odell *et al* (1993) indicated that if catheter size exceeds this recommendation or if the procedure is unduly prolonged, hypoxaemia and damage to the integrity of the mucosal wall will develop. Whereas Czarnick *et al* (1991) noted that there were no differences in the amount of trauma, tissue ulceration and necrosis caused when either continuous or intermittent suctioning was performed. They recommended that the practice of 1–2 hourly suctioning should be kept to a minimum or based on the assessment of need.

For ventilator-dependent patients or those who are cardiovascularly unstable, pre-oxygenation with 100% oxygen for 2–3 minutes is advocated before suctioning as is manual hyperinflation with a rebreathing bag. These techniques will provide lung expansion and prevent desaturation post-suctioning (Odell *et al*, 1993; Stacy, 1996). However Clapham, Harrison and Raybould (1995) advocate that training in hyperinflation is vital and is the assessement of the patient's tidal volumes to ensure that volume requirements can be met during manual bagging. A more recent innovation that helps to reduce the occurrence of hypoxaemic episodes and cardiovascular instability is the use of a closed-system multipleuse suction catheter (Redick, 1993). The closed system of suctioning also has the advantage of helping to maintain levels of arterial oxygenation because it reduces the loss of ventilatory positive end expiratory pressure (PEEP) which, in turn, serves to keep the alveoli distended. Further, the use of this system can minimise bacterial contamination of patients, staff and surrounding area which can be caused each time the respiratory circuit is disconnected which is typical of single use systems.

The most common risks associated with suctioning include hypoxaemia, cardiac dysrhythmias, pain, discomfort, stress, infection and damage to the lining of the mucosa which with repeated insults, can cause necrosis and the formation of fissures. Many of the complications can be avoided by adhering to the key principles and implementation of research based protocols. The management of the patient can be further enhanced by administration of analgesia and by providing regular explanations on all aspects of their treatment.

Regarding frequency of suctioning, there is at present some debate within the literature. Rudy *et al*, (1991) suggest that frequent endotracheal suctioning in patients with severe head injury can raise the mean intracranial pressure (ICP) and cerebral hypertension with dangerous consequences. The cumulative response of repeated suction sequences is a delay in neurological recovery due to an increase of tissue oedema caused by an elevation of pressure in the cerebral capillaries. However, to lessen the deleterious effects of the peaks and of rising mean ICP as noted in patients, it is suggested that nurses limit the suction procedure to two ETT passes per session and that the patient should be preoxygenated prior to this (Rudy *et al*, 1991).

Others suggest that suctioning should be performed only when neccessary thereby limiting the number of catheter passes (Maninelli-Van Atta and Beck, 1992; Odell *et al*, 1993). Frequency should be determined by factors relating either to the evaluation of secretions (for example purulence and viscocity), airway status or as a result of changes in the patient's condition. It is advocated that due to the complexity of decisions required in relation to ETT suctioning, nurses must carefully assess each patient and plan their strategies according to need and not on the basis of routine (Copnell and Fergusson,1995).

Another area of controversy concerns the installation of saline into the ETT to help loosen pulmonary secretions, a practice that seems to have survived on apparent logic and anecdotal evidence. A decade ago Ackerman (1985) reasoned that there was no benefit for the continuance of administering 3–10 mls of normal saline down a patient's airway. It has been suggested that the installation of saline can irritate the mucosa of the trachea and can interfere with the exchange of gases within the alveoli (Odell *et al*, 1993; Hooper, 1996). More recently, Raymond's (1995) review of the literature concluded that there is a lack of scientific studies to support the routine installation of normal saline into the ETT and therefore this should be abandoned.

The final aspect relating to the maintenance of the airway is ensuring that the tube is well secured and strapped to the patient in order to prevent slipping or trauma. Unless the ETT is firmly secured it may migrate downwards, commonly into the right bronchus causing lung collapse and complications in the left lung. It is equally likely that the airway may be dislodged upwards, resulting in extubation, irritant cough or damage to the vocal chords (Ashurst, 1997a). Patient comfort can be achieved by using foam padding around the tapes and supporting the ventilatory circuit with available frameworks can also minimise distress or injury. Nurses should record the position of the tube at the mouth/nose and document this at the end of every shift, as this will provide evidence of subtle displacement. Cuff-management is equally vital in protecting the patient from the aspiration of gastric contents and serves to anchor the tube in place. Over inflation, however, can lead to necrosis, the cuff may equally herniate and obstruct the airway, thus regular checking of cuff pressure is a vital element of the nurse's role (Stacy, 1996).

Promoting oxygenation

Many critically-ill patients with respiratory failure will be dependent on high concentrations of inspired oxygen therapy to maintain adequate arterial oxygenation, unless they have a chronic respiratory condition.

Atmospheric room oxygen (O_2) is 21% and in health is sufficient to produce a sufficient gradient for the transfer of this gas into the arterial circulation and to maintain cellular functioning. However, the transfer of O_2 may be affected by the thickness of the wall membranes, the degree of dead space and reduced lung compliance. Nurses need to be cognisant with the factors which impede the transport of gases in the critically ill patient in order that further adverse effects may be prevented.

While O_2 is necessary for cellular survival, inspired concentrations of greater than 50% for more than a twenty-four hour period, can be detrimental in producing diffuse alveolar damage and pulmonary oxygen toxicity (Balentine, 1982; Stacy, 1996). Many of the changes are reversible within days of stopping or decreasing the levels of inspired oxygen. Despite this O_2 therapy remains a mainstay in the management of patients with respiratory failure but the concentration delivered needs regular appraisal.

There are, however, other manoeuvres that are also utilised to enrich patient's oxygenation and can assist in reducing the amount of inspired O_2. The use of PEEP for example increases the functional residual capacity of the lungs by opening and recruiting alveoli. Moreover, by distending previously collapsed alveoli PEEP increases the available surface area for the diffusion of gases and reduces intra-pulmonary shunting, (Hillman, 1986). Despite this, there are problems relating to high levels of PEEP, ie. >15cm of H_2O (Oh, 1988). With an increase in intra-thoracic pressure the patient becomes at risk from barotrauma and surgical emphysema. Further, this rise in pressure reduces venous return and elevates pulmonary vascular resistance which, in turn, raises afterload in the right ventricle resulting in a low cardiac output as well as decreased urinary output. For many patients these cardiovascular effects may compromise their condition further. Cerebral oedema is also likely because venous blood draining downwards has to overcome the raised pressure in the thoracic cavity, which can lead to congestion as well as high ICP readings (Hillman, 1986). In combination both oxygen therapy and PEEP have traditionally reflected the medical management to acute respiratory failure, although it has been pointed out that very little attention has been given by nurses to the role of positioning of the patient as means of optimising PO_2 (Albarran, 1992; Tyler, 1984).

For some time now it has been established that the appropriate choice of patient posture can optimise arterial oxygen in those with unilateral or bilateral lung disease (Zack *et al*, 1974; Ibanez *et al*, 1981; Rivara *et al*, 1984). These investigators demonstrated that significant changes in PO_2 were achieved when mechanically ventilated patients with one-sided lung disease were nursed with their sick lung uppermost. By comparison, these benefits decreased when the healthy lung was uppermost and when the patients were nursed in the supine position. Banasik *et al*, (1987) similarly described how a group of 60 adult cardiac surgery patients who were mechanically ventilated had a statistically higher level of arterial oxygenation while lying on the right lateral position. However, when lying in the left lateral position a lower PO_2 was noted. The rationale for this change is because during heart surgery the left lung is temporarily collapsed and handled, thus at greater risk of atelectasis.

The explanation for an improvement of arterial PO_2, relates to the manipulation of blood flow by means of gravitational forces and the distribution of higher tidal ventilation volumes in the dependent lung zones (West, 1990). Employing lateral positioning allows blood flow to be directed towards the unaffected lung, where ventilation is optimal thus assisting to reduce the degree of pulmonary shunting. In addition Demers (1987) notes that in health, the distribution of tidal ventilation favours the dependent lung because of differences in pleural pressures and in the number of alveoli which equate to as much as 3½ of the pulmonary volume, whereas the share of perfusion, can be as much as 18 times greater in the dependent lung when compared to an upper region. It is not surprising then that placing patients with the good lung down is advantageous. The implication of these findings for nurses are that they must select the most favourable positions that will not only be of benefit to the patient in terms of oxygenation but will also provide comfort and protection to the skin from damage. In addition the patient's posture should be correlated with the arterial blood gases (ABGs) and documented on the notes and charts. This will minimise the potential for erroneous decisions that may be made on an assessment of ABGs.

In contrast, the use of the prone position, first advocated over two decades ago (Bryan, 1974), as a strategy for improving PO_2 in patients with acute bilateral lung disease, pneumonia and ARDS is gaining much attention (Albarran, 1992; Brüssel *et al*, 1993; Broccard *et al*, 1997; Gaussorges *et al*, 1987; Pappert *et al*, 1994; Ryan and Pelosi, 1996). The suggested mechanisms for improvements in arterial oxygenation arising from the prone position include:

- improvements in functional residual capacity (FRC)
- increased drainage of secretions
- a redistribution of perfusion to the ventral lung zones
- changes of regional ventilation and redistribution of ventilation (Kesecioglu, 1997; Pappert *et al*, 1994).

As a result of these factors, ventilation-perfusion mismatch is reversed. This is further improved as a result of a recruitment of previously collapsed dorsal alveoli as well as due to greater changes in diaphragmatic movement that are unimpeded by abdominal contents. Consequently reducing the detrimental levels of inspired oxygen and of PEEP is feasible.

In this posture, the patients cardiovascular state appears to stabilise and they can tolerate tracheal suctioning without precipitating dysrhythmias (Brüssel *et al*, 1993 Langer *et al*, 1988). However, experience and research suggests that the substantial increments in arterial oxygenation appear to be sustained for a only short a period once patients are nursed in the conventional positions, although in many cases the PaO_2 remains above pre-prone values (Albarran, 1995; Brüssell *et al*, 1993; Douglas *et al*, 1977; Langer *et al*, 1988). Langer *et al*, (1988) have also suggested that a lack of response after half-hour of pronation is an index as to whether the patient will improve from being nursed in this way, and there does appear to be a small group of non-responders in most of the available studies.

When using the prone position, one pillow must be in

place at the upper end of the thorax and another below the stomach, thus allowing for the abdomen to drop downwards and thus preventing compression of the lungs. Also, from a practical point specific areas for nursing attention are the groin areas, forehead, breasts and knees as they are at risk of pressure sore development. Periorbital oedema is also a likely complication (Brüssel *et al*, 1993) so patients should be nursed with the head of the bed slightly up (Albarran, 1995; Canter, 1987). Additionally, the airway should be well secured and, prior to turning the patients should be given a bolus of sedation and analgesia. It may be necessary to disconnect less vital infusion lines before the procedure. Because the change in posture involves promoting pulmonary drainage regular suctioning may be required. It is speculated that this helps the recruitment of dorsal alveoli thereby assisting to raise PO_2. However, the risk of the ET airway blocking may occur if the secretions which are draining are thick and viscous, and have not been adequately humidified. Other possible complications include migration of the ET tube into the right main bronchus, veno-caval obstruction and retinal damage. Finally, what seems important with regards to the prone position is the early intervention and implementation of this option for selected patients, although further work is required.

Inhaled nitric oxide (NO) has also gained popularity as a measure for reducing pulmonary hypertension and for augmenting gas exchange (Bender *et al*, 1997; Evans and Sair, 1995; Greenough, 1995; Woodrow, 1997). NO is found naturally in the endothelial cells and undergoes a process which culminates in arterial muscle relaxation. Because NO diffuses easily into cells it can regulate the amount of blood flow through tissue or organ. It has now been established that an inhaled preparation can be used in an acute respiratory illness to reduce pulmonary vascular resistance, redirecting blood to the ventilated alveoli thereby decreasing the degree of intra-pulmonary shunt and right sided ventricular pressures (Bender *et al*, 1997; Evans and Sair, 1995). However, the wide use of inhaled NO in clinical practice requires further evaluation and there are concerns over potential implications for haemodynamic functioning and possible side effects, many of which are still unkown, as well as issues of storage and safety problems (Eichacker, 1997; Warren and Higenbottam, 1996).

Monitoring respiratory progress and comfort

Benner (1984) has identified that one of the core competencies of expert practitioners is the skill of rapidly discerning subtle changes in a patient's condition. With regards to the patient requiring MV, there are a number of observations that need to be monitored. These include, mode of ventilation, level of inspired O_2, the amount of volume the patient is receiving per breath (tidal volume), respiratory movements, breathing pattern, breath sounds and minute volume as well as the degree of inspiratory pressure required to inflate the lungs (Rainbow, 1989; Robb, 1993). A change in one or more of these variables can be an index of whether the patient's ventilation is improving, adequate or worsening, it therefore seems appropriate to consider the monitoring of the respiratory parameters as central to the nurse's role. Ashurst (1997b) suggests that ventilator alarms should be cautiously set so that extreme fluctuations may be rapidly detected and initiate appropriate action.

The methods of delivering oxygen and air to a mechanically ventilated patient and for weaning respiratory support are becoming more diverse and sophisticated in that they can be tailored to the individual's clinical condition (Aloi and Burns, 1995; Broiness, 1992; Richless, 1993; Vasbinder-Dillon, 1988). Rainbow (1989) and Robb (1993) provide a detailed account of the relevant respiratory observations and likely causes that may trigger alarms which can aid the nurse to the identify the problem. However not all problems are solved this way, and it is often the patient who may give the nurse a clue by the way the accessory muscles move with each inspiration or by their distressed appearance, events that may occur before any alarms sound.

Part of the monitoring dimension of the nurse caring for the MV patient is the analysis of arterial blood gases (ABGs). The results of a sample obtained from the arterial catheter, give an indication as to the effectiveness of respiratory therapy and gas exchange (Tasota and Wesmiller, 1994). Interpretation must not be considered in isolation and should include evaluation of ventilator settings and the position of the patient as, without evaluation of these aspects, it is very likely that the judgement on the patient's blood gas may be erroneous.

The analysis of arterial blood gases needs to be

systematic and based on five main steps, these include pH, partial pressure of arterial carbon dioxide $PaCO_2$ as well as PaO_2, level of standard bicarbonate and the degree of physiological compensation (Tasota and Wesmiller, 1994). Each of these measures will point to changes within the patient's respiration or metabolic state as reflected by alterations in acid-base balance. As well as evaluating the ABGs, care of the arterial line must be a priority since it is a highly invasive procedure which provides not only a route for sampling of blood but for continuous arterial pressure monitoring. The likelihood of the arterial catheter becoming disconnected, or accidentally removed also places the patient in jeopardy as a result of haemorrhaging. Thus, the arterial site must be visible and checked regularly.

Currently the use of pulse oximetry has also become established as a tool for monitoring arterial haemoglobin oxygen saturation in ventilated and weaning patients. This is because the measure provides a continuous and rapid indicator of either poor gas exchange or response to therapy (Coull, 1992; Sonnesso, 1991) and has served to alert staff to a patients' improper position (Hovagim *et al*, 1989; Lasater-Erhard, 1995). Once it is confirmed that changes in pulse oxymetry are genuine this should direct the nurse to obtain an ABG and/or take appropriate action. As Sonnesso (1991) suggests, deteriorating trends can thus be spotted and intercepted by the nurse.

As important as the above, is the assessment and monitoring of the patients' comfort and desired depth of sedation. Presently, the available scales can provide a guide to optimal levels of consciouness required, ensuring that dosages are kept to a minimum, thereby avoiding short and long term adverse effects associated with sedative agents (Creasy, 1996; Laing, 1992; Westcott, 1995). The routine use of sedation during a period of MV is a practice undertaken for humanistic reasons. However maintaining and achieving this is a complex issue which demands a systematic and multi-disciplinary approach. Careful titration of an infusion or small bolus doses of sedation with analgesia can achieve much. This includes ensuring patient comfort, helping to minimise environmental psychosis, enabling control levels, intracranial pressures, toleration of the ETT and co-operation with the ventilator mode. In addition, nursing procedures or physiotherapy may also be performed without causing much distress (Creasy, 1996; Laing, 1992; Westcott, 1995). While the available sedation scales are far from perfect, their use in combination with analgesia, verbal communication and caring touch can serve to enhance the quality of patient care and minimise the problems of under and oversedation that has been observed in the past. Nurses must also ensure that the patient has planned periods of uninterrupted sleep. This may involve developing specific strategies commencing with examining the use of sedation and documentation policies, monitoring the effects of environmental noise pollutants as well as the necessity and frequency of nursing interventions (Evans and French, 1995; Finlay, 1991; Parker, 1995). Critically ill patients require sustained periods of quality sleep in order to promote physical and emotional recuperation, recovery and well being.

Because many ventilated patients are vulnerable and unconscious, they are dependant on nurses to identify and prevent potential complications resulting from MV or from associated treatments, many of which have already been mentioned. Respiratory, cardiovascular and gastro-intestinal complications are well documented as are disturbances in acid-base balance, fluid and electrolytes (Hillman, 1986; Ponte, 1990; Vasbinder-Dillon, 1988). Arguably, the use of positioning, humidification, suctioning, sedation scoring, oxygen therapy and the monitoring of pertinent parameters can all contribute significantly to preventing and limiting the number of problems for the patient while on MV, and therefore can all be conceived as key nursing priorities of care. Underpinning the nurse's role must be maintaining the safety of the patient throughout their stay in intensive care. Their families must be kept sufficiently informed with regards to the patients' progress/condition as well as all aspects of nursing interventions, that may even include involving them in delivering direct care if and when appropriate.

Safe and uncomplicated weaning of ventilator

Traditionally most of the nursing priorities for the MV patient have been focused on the acute situation and on day to day care. However, it is advanced that it is nurses who should be implementing strategies that will facilitate rapid and uncomplicated weaning from MV. According to Armstrong (1995) and Petty (1995) it is not uncommon for the weaning process to be lengthy and when compounded by setbacks it can demotivate patient, families and staff alike. It may thus be reasoned that the outcome in the transition from assisted respiratory support to spontaneous ventilation, in part depends on correcting the underlying pathology which precipitated the need for intubation and MV, (Armstrong, 1995; Weilitz, 1993) but, in part, it also relies on the emotional support and motivation that nurses provide that inspires the patient's confidence.

In deciding whether a patient is ready to be weaned and extubated comprehensive assessment of the following areas is mandatory:

- respiratory parameters
- metabolic criteria
- cardiovascular functioning
- neurological evaluation
- psychological readiness.

Recently, Clement and Buck (1996) have suggested that there is confusion regarding the definitions of successful weaning. Bridges (1992) alternatively claims that many of the respiratory measures used to decide a patient's readiness for extubation, like maximal voluntary ventilation (MVV), have not been systematically validated nor are they accurate in forecasting successful weaning of MV. Moreover, many are unwieldy or too complex to be carried out at the bedside, and depend on much co-operation from the patient.

However, the most cited criteria which focus on the mechanics of ventilation and that are used in practice are the patient's ability to cough and co-operate with the nursing staff/physiotherapist, the presence of bilateral air entry, as well as the individual being able to fulfil the following:

Table 1.2: Respiratory parameters to assss for in planning extubation

Mechanical variables	Gas exchange criteria
Minute volume: 10 litres or less	• pH that ranges between 7.35 and 7.45 and compensating
Respiratory rate:< 25 breaths per minute	
Breathing not laboured	
Tidal volume: > 5mls/kg	$PaO_{2>}$10Kpa (80mmHg) with an FiO_2 of <0.5 **or**
PEEP: 5cm H_2O or less (if ventilated)	$PaO_{2>}$8Kpa (60mmHg) with an FiO_2 of <0.4
(Clement and Buck, 1996; Hinds and Watson, 1996)	(Clement and Buck, 1996; Hinds and Watson, 1996; Weilitz, 1993)

Collectively, these more common measures provide evidence of pulmonary functioning, reserve and endurance, which are vital for optimal weaning. Haemodynamic observations, blood gases and pulse oximetry measures must be obtained and recorded as they serve as indices of gas exchange and will guide nursing management of the patient. Caution is necessary when applying these parameters to those with chronic obstructive airway disease, particularly with reference to arterial oxygen levels as they will be accustomed to abnormal baseline values, unlike patients with acute illness, and correcting these may depress spontaneous breathing (Clochesy *et al*, 1995; Knebel, 1991; Weilitz, 1993).

The choice of weaning modes available within a ventilator are diverse and important as they play a role in facilitating the transition from artificial to spontaneous ventilation. The more common include, synchronised intermittent mandatory ventilation (SIMV), pressure support (PS) ventilation, continuous positive airway pressure (CPAP), all of which can be applied as individual modes or as combined (Ashford, 1990; Clement and Buck, 1996; Weilitz, 1993). More recently, biphasic positive airway pressure (BiPAP) has been introduced. This is a technique which relies on two levels of airway pressure that are delivered through a standard ventilator by means of a face/nose mask, (Kiehl *et al*, 1996). For intubated patients a higher level of airway pressure is supplied during inspiration and the lower during expiration, cycling may be controlled by intermittent switching between the two levels of CPAP, while permitting the patient to spontaneously breathe at any phase of the respiratory cycle. Respiratory rates can also be regulated by altering the inspiratory-expiratory (I:E) ratio as in controlled ventilation or set according to the individual's clinical state. Kiehl *et al*, (1996) report that the advantage of this technique is that it limits peak inspiratory pressure overcoming the risks of lung injury such as barotrauma and surgical emphysema. In addition, the benefits in gas exchange permit a reduction of the inspired oxygen. Burns *et al*, (1995) add that BiPaP (via face mask) may obviate the need for conventional intubation and benefit those with chronic cardiac or pulmonary difficulties since they can be managed more easily, presumably because there are less physiological demands. As such, it has been proposed that the scope of non-invasive positive pressure ventilation (NIPPV) will increase because it is thought to be safe and effective in the management of patients with acute respiratory failure. As well as being less costly, newer respiratory modes seem to be better tolerated and are associated with less complications (Abou-Shala and Meduri, 1996; Dinner and Goldstone, 1997). Despite these advantages, the patient who is confused and hypoxic may not cope or endure a face mask.

During the weaning of patients, nurses must evaluate how the individual responds to a reduction in the level of pulmonary assistance while on the ventilator (such as a lowering of PEEP to 5 cm H_2O, the number of preset breaths or positive airway pressure) or whether the patient is coping with spontaneous breathing with a T-piece, and humidified oxygen. Monitoring the patient's response will assist in judging whether the process of extubation will need to be gentle or speedy. Progressing to early extubation or to a T-piece following a short period of ventilatory support will be far easier for those who have been on MV for a couple of days or less (Clement and Buck, 1996; Weilitz, 1993). Traditionally, the patient who had been dependent on respiratory support for a prolonged period would commence with brief periods of spontaneous breathing through a T-piece interchanging this assisted ventilation, a very lengthy process. However NIPPV can facilitate safe weaning of respiratory support and reduce the duration of this stage when compared to conventional methods (Dinner and Goldstone, 1997).

For patients who may require long-term ventilation or with an upper airway obstruction, a percutaneous tracheostomy may be created as it facilitates weaning and the removal of secretions, reduces the amount of dead space, is more comfortable and less distressing for the patient. In addition, it is also possible for patients to talk and eat with adjustment to the tracheostomy tube. Although the risks of infection, trauma, accidental displacement, surgical emphysema and scarring are also significant (Ashurst, 1997a; Stacy, 1996). In decreasing dependency on the ventilator, the principles regarding the weaning process stated above apply for the patient with a tracheostomy.

Metabolic assessment

Metabolic evaluation is concerned with establishing whether the nutritional intake corresponds with demands, this is of importance for the intensive care patient who may have higher requirements due to his/her clinical condition, (Armstrong, 1995; Weilitz, 1993). In order to restore respiratory function and promote the process of weaning, the dietary plan must be tailored to reflect the individual's needs. For example, a high intake of carbohydrates when metabolised will increase the amount of circulating carbon dioxide which, in turn, will trigger hyper-ventilation in order to correct the acid-base imbalance, but is likely to exhaust the patient. Alternatively, insufficient nutrition or starvation results in a breakdown of skeletal muscle and other tissues utilising protein and energy reserves which in turn cause expenditure of precious oxygen reserves in these compromised patients. Low phosphates too, produce many physiological changes of which muscle weakness and reduced diaphragmatic functioning are typical and a deficiency may lead to respiratory failure (Aubier *et al*,1985; Lewis *et al*, 1987). Additionally, if hypophosphataemia is not managed it will inevitably delay the weaning of patients from MV due to impaired contractility of diaphragm and pulmonary muscles, thus, this like others electrolytes needs to be monitored and corrected as necessary. Similarly, Clochesy *et al* (1995) found that in their work with chronically ill patients requiring weaning, those with a higher than normal serum albumin and lower respiratory rates returned to spontaneous breathing sooner and experienced lower rates of mortality. It is suggested that in the presence of a low serum albumin, hydrostatic pressure exceeds the reduced colloidal osmotic pressure and this leads to pulmonary oedema. There is undoubtedly a relationship between nutritional status and respiratory muscle energy and nurses seem to recognise that feeding is an early priority of care as it appears a crucial factor in terms of patient outcome (Clement and Buck, 1996; Jenny and Logan, 1994).

Cardiovascular parameters

Successful weaning also depends on assessing the cardiac status of the patient. According to Armstrong (1995) and Hinds and Watson (1996) a raised blood pressure, dysrhythmias and a low haemoglobin of less than 10g/dl will compromise cardiac output and oxygen transport and thus jeopardise the weaning stages. In addition, the presence of left ventricular failure (LVF) may delay the weaning process (Clochesy *et al*, 1995). Nonetheless, these investigators also report that patients with heart failure who are managed aggressively with medications to improve left ventricular function are weaned more successfully than those who are treated conservatively. Additionally, Clochesy *et al*, (1995) noted that those in which weaning is delayed are often overloaded by a litre or more and therefore they advocate that a goal of treatment should include an even or negative balance if weaning is planned. Whereas Hurford and Favorito (1995) have observed that the presence of ischaemia on the ECG is associated with a failure to wean from MV, Edwards and Hess (1996) also advise that for post-operative cardiac surgery patients with a low cardiac index, and a blood loss greater than 150mls/hour for two consecutive hours into the chest drains, continuing the period of post-operative ventilation is appropriate for controlling myocardial ischaemia. Furthermore, in these patients normothermia is also desirable as is a chest drainage loss of 50 mls/hour or less. It is currently emphasised that adherence to rigorous nursing protocols can contribute to ensuring to safety and high standards of care in weaning patients from MV (Clement and Buck, 1996; Edwards and Hess, 1996) as well as in assisting with demarcating the boundaries of professional activity (Davies, 1997).

Neurological evaluation

The other area to examine prior to extubation is neurological functioning (Armstrong, 1995; Knebel, 1991). This should focus on ascertaining a patients' level of alertness and whether pain is under control as this may impede rational thinking. Patients may be reluctant to collaborate either with deep breathing, expanding their chest fully or with coughing, due to their pain. In some patients evidence of hypoxaemia, cerebral irritation or over sedation will inhibit co-operation with staff, this may delay the decision to instigate weaning. While not all patients may be fully orientated, as long as they have a cough and gag reflex, or there is evidence in the form of behaviour that they object to the ETT, this may be sufficient to commence weaning. Assessment of patients should include direct and indirect parameters of cognitive state. For example, the clearance rate of sedative agents can be influential (Edwards and Hess, 1996), as well as how a patient responds to staff communication, degree of restless-ness and whether the individual is able to focus on their breathing (Jenny and Logan, 1994). These factors should all be considered as they also play a key role in deciding whether to commence weaning.

Psychological readiness

Anxiety, lack of sleep and fear of pain may inhibit under-standing of a patient and this may influence the commitment and attitude towards participating in the weaning process. It is thus essential that as well as having their pain controlled, planned periods of rest, avoiding fatigue, a safe environment, regular explanations should be given, so that the patient is emotionally prepared to cope confidently with returning to spontaneous respiration (Petty, 1995; Jenny and Logan, 1994). The content of communication should be focused on the procedures involved, how their breathing will feel once extubated and what to do if distressed (Knebel, 1991). Interactions should also be directed at managing the patient's concerns, promoting collaboration, and in strengthening the nurse-patient relationship, as it is this that is a first and foremost priority in effectively caring for those with MV. Jenny and Logan (1994) also feel that nurses must engage the patient's trust as this will further facilitate the withdrawal of MV and restore independent functioning.

Psychological readiness of the patient for weaning is more of a qualitative measure, but nurses by virtue of their close contact and observations 'know' their patients (Jenny and Logan, 1994). These authors describe how nurses estimated their patient's preparedness for weaning, this entailed assessing the amount of work and energy that they devoted to breathing (Jenny and Logan, 1994). Other aspects included whether the patient was able concentrate on specific respiratory tasks, the willingness of individuals to assume decisions and take control of their care. Moreover it is claimed, that it is the skills, experience and additional education of nurses that has a significant influence on the duration and success of weaning patients from MV who are suffering with a chronic respiratory illness (Petty, 1995; Thorens *et al*, 1995). It is suggested that this is due to mastery in being able to discriminate and select the relevant patient data to prioritise nursing interventions which will optimise recovery and minimise complications.

Table 1.3: Complications associated with mechanical ventilation

Cardiovascular:	decreases venous return decreases cardiac output dysrhythmias
Respiratory:	barotrauma pulmonary oedema tension pneumothorax V/Q inequalities surgical emphysema atelectasis tracheal damage (necrosis/burns/fissure) hypo/hyperventilation pulmonary oxygen toxicity upper/lower airway infections obstructed airway
Gastro-intestinal:	pulmonary aspiration stress ulcers gastric distension paralytic ileus malnutrition
Other:	nosocomial infections fluid and electrolyte imbalance
Equipment failure:	accidental disconnection undetected leaks faulty endotracheal tube bacterial contamination of circuit and ventilator system

References

Abou-shala N, Meduri GU (1996) Non-invasive mechanical ventilation in patients with acute respiratory failure. *Crit Care Med* **24**(4): 705–715

Ackerman MH (1993) The effect of saline lavage prior to suctioning. *Am J Nurs* **2**(4) 326–330

Albarran JW (1991) A review of communication with intubated patients and those with tracheostomies within an intensive care environment. *Inten Care Nurs* **7**(3): 179–186

Albarran JW (1992) *The prone position: An alternative to improving arterial oxygenation— A critical review of the published literature.* Unpublished BSc (Hons) Disseration,

University of the West of England, Bristol

Albarran JW (1995) *The prone position as an alternative for improving PaO₂— A nursing strategy?* University of Glasgow, BACCN 10th annual conference

Aloi A, Burns S (1995) Continuous airway pressure monitoring in the critical care setting. *Crit Care Nurs* **15**: 66–75

Armstrong M (1995) Preparing to breathe alone. *Nurs Times* **91**(38): 53–56

Ashurst S (1992) Suction therapy in the critically ill patient. *Br J Nurs* **1**(10): 485–489

Ashurst S (1997a) Nursing care of the mechanically ventilated patient in ITU:1. *Br J Nurs* **6**(8): 447–453

Ashurst S (1997b) Nursing care of the mechanically ventilated patient in ITU:2. *Br J Nurs* **6**(9): 475–485

Ashford L (1990) Pressure support ventilation. *Crit Care Nurs* **10**(7): 20–279

Aubier M, Murciano D, Lecoguic Y et al (1985) Effect of hypophosphatemia on diaphragmatic contractility in patients with acute respiratory failure. *N Engl J Med* **313**: 420–424

Ballard K, Cheesman T, Ripiner T et al (1992) Humidification for ventilated patients. *Inten Cri Care Nurs* **8**(1): 2–9

Balentine JD (1982) *Pathology of oxygen toxicity*. Academic Press, Harcourt Brace Jovanovich Publishers, New York

Banasik JL, Bruya M, Steadman R et al(1987) Effect of position on arterial oxygenation in postoperative coronary revascularisation patients. *Heart and Lung* **16**(6): 652–657

Bender K, Alexander J, Enos J et al (1997) Effects of inhaled nitric oxide in patients with hypoxaemia and pulmonary hypertension after cardiac surgery. *Am J Crit Care* **6**(2): 127–131

Benner P (1984) *From novice to expert: Excellence and Power in Clinical Nursing*. Addison-Wesley Publishing Company, Menlo Park

Branson RD, Chatburn RL (1993) Humidification of inspired gases during mechanical ventilation. *Respir Care* **38**(5): 461–467

Branson RD, Davis K, Brown R et al (1996) Comparison of three humidification techniques during mechanical ventilation: Patient selection, cost and infection considerations. *Respir Care* **41**(9): 809–816

Bridges EJ (1992) Transition from ventilatory support:Knowing when the patient is ready to wean. *Crit Care Nurs Quarterly* **15**(1): 14–20

Brioness TL (1992) Pressure support ventilation: New ventilatory technique. *Crit Care Nurs* **12**(4): 51–58

Broccard A, Shapiro R, Schmitz L et al(1997) Influence of the prone position on the extent and distribution of lung injury in high tidal volume oleic acid model of acute respiratory distress syndrome. *Crit Care Med* **25**: 16–27

Brüsell T, Hanchenberg T, Roos N et al (1993) Mechanical ventilation in the prone position for acute respiratory failure after cardiac surgery. *J Cardiothorac Vasc Anes* **7**(5): 541–546

Bryan AC (1974) Comments of a devil's advocate. *Am Rev Respir Dis* **110**: 143–144

Burns S, Clochesy J, Hanneman S *et al*(1995) Weaning from long-term mechanical ventilation. *Am J Crit Care* **4**(1): 4–22

Canter C (1987) Nursing mechanically ventilated patients in the prone position. *Care Crit Ill* **3**(3): 70–71

Clapham L, Harrison J, Raybould T (1995) A multi-disciplinary audit of manual hyperinflation technique (sigh breath) in a neurosurgical intensive care unit. *Inten Crit Care Nurs* **11**(5): 265–271

Clement JM, Buck A (1996) Weaning from mechanical ventilatory support. *Dimensions Crit Care Nurs* **15**(3): 114–129

Clochesy J, Daly B, Montenegro H (1995) Weaning chronically ill adults from mechanical ventilatory support: a descriptive study. *Am J Nurs* **4**(2): 93–99

Copnell B, Fergusson D (1995) Endotracheal suctioning: Time-worn ritual or timely intervention? *Am J Nurs* **4**(2): 100–105

Coull A (1992) Making sense of pulse oxymetry. *Nurs Times* **88**(32): 42–43

Cutcliffe J (1996) Critically ill patient's perspectives of hope. *Br J Nurs* **5**(11): 674–690

Creasy J (1996) Sedation scoring: assessment tools. *Nurs Crit Care* **1**(4): 171–177

Czarnick R, Stone K, Everhart C *et al*(1991) Differential effects of continuous versus intermittent suction on tracheal tissue. *Heart Lung* **20**(2): 144–151

Davies N (1997) Nurse-initiated extubation following cardiac surgery. *Inten Crit Care Nurs* **13**(2): 77–79

Demers RR (1987) Down with the good lung. *Respir Care* **32**(10): 849–850

Dinner L, Goldstone JC (1997) Non-invasive ventilation in the intensive care unit and operating theatre. *Br J Hosp Med* **57**(3): 91–94

Douglas W, Rehder K, Beynen M *et al* (1977) Improved oxygenation in patients with acute respiratory failure: The prone position. *Am Rev Respir Dis* **115**: 559–565

Dyer I (1995a) Preventing the ITU syndrome or how not to torture an ITU patient, part 1. *Inten Crit Care Nurs* **11**(4): 130–139

Dyer I (1995b) Preventing the ITU syndrome or how not to torture an ITU patient, part 2. *Inten Crit Care Nurs* **11**(4): 223–232

Edwards D, Hess L (1996) Aggressive weaning in cardiac surgical patients. *Dimensions Crit Care Nurs* **14**(4): 181–186

EichackerPQ (1997) Inhaled nitric oxide in adult respiratory distress syndrome: Do we know the risks versus benefits.

Crit Care Med **25**(4): 563–565

Evans T, Sair M (1995) Nitric oxide-thoughts for the future. *Care Crit Ill* **11**(4): 136–137

Evans J, French D (1995) Sleep and healing in intensive care settings. *Dimensions Crit Care Nurs* **14**(4): 189–199

Finlay G (1991) Sleep and intensive care. *Inten Care Nurs* **7**(1): 61–68

Fiorentini A (1992) Potential hazards of tracheobronchial suctioning. *Inten Crit Care Nurs* **8**(4): 217–226

Gaussorgues P, Chazot C, Vendrinne C *et al* (1987) Amelioration des pneumopathies diffuses par la ventilation en decubitus ventral. *La Presse Medicale* **16**(24): 1200

Greenough A (1995) Nitric oxide- clinical aspects. *Care Crit Ill* **11**(4): 143–146

Hinds CJ, Watson D (1996) *Intensive Care: A concise textbook*, (2nd edition). WB Saunders Co Ltd, London

Hillman DR (1986) Physiological aspects of intermittent positive pressure ventilation. *Anaes Inten Care* **14**: 226–235

Hovagim A, Backus W, Manecke G *et al*(1989) Pulse oxymetry and patient positioning: A report of eight cases. *Anaesthesiol* **71**(3): 454–456

Hooper M (1996) Nursing care of the patient with a tracheostomy. *Nurs Stan* **10**(34): 40–43

Hurford W, Favorito F (1995) Association of myocardial ischaemia with failure to wean from mechanical ventilation. *Crit Care Med* **23**: 1475–1480

Ibanez J, Raurich M, Abizanda R *et al*(1981) The effect of lateral positions on gas exchange in patients with unilateral lung disease during mechanical ventilation. *Inten Care Med* **7**: 231–234

Jackson C (1996) Humidification in the upper respiratory tract: a physiological overview. *Inten Crit Care Nurs* **12**: 27–32

Jenny J, Logan J (1994) Promoting ventilator independence: *A gorunded theory perspective*. Dimensions Crit Care Nurs **13**(1): 29–37

Joynt G, Lipman J, (1994) The use of heat and moisture exchangers in critically ill patients. *Care Crit Ill* **10**(6): 271–275

Keihl M, Schiele C, Stenzinger W *et al* (1996) Volume-controlled versus biphasisc positive airway pressure ventilation in leukopaenic patients with severe respiratory failure. *Crit Care Med* **24**(5): 780–784

Kesecioglu J (1997) Prone position in therapy-refractory hypoxaemia. *Curr Opin Anaes* **10**: 92–100

Knebel AR (1991) Weaning from mechanical ventilation: Current controversies. *Heart Lung* **20**: 321–334

Laing A (1992) The applicability of new sedation scale for intensive care. *Inten Crit Care Nurs* **8**(3): 149–152

Langer M, Mascheroni D, Marcolin R *et al* (1988) The prone position in ARDS patients. *Chest* **94**(1): 103–107

Lasater-Erhard M (1995) The effect of position on arterial oxygen saturation. *Crit Care Nurse* **15**: 31–36

Lewis J, Hodsman A, Driedger A *et al* (1987) Hypophosphatemia and respiratory failure: Prolonged abnormal energy metabolism demonstrated by nuclear magnetic resonance spectroscopy. *Am J Med* **83**: 1139–1143

Maninelli Van Atta J, Beck S (1992) Preventing hypoxaemia and haemodynamic compromise related to endotracheal suctioning. *Am J Crit Care* **1**: 62

Martin C, Perrin G, Gevaudan MJ *et al* (1990) Heat and moisture exchangers and vaporising humidifiers in the intensive care unit. *Chest* **97**: 144–149

McEvoy M, Carey T (1995) Shivering and rewarming after cardiac surgery: comparison of ventilator circuits with humidifier and heated wires and moisture exchangers. *Am J Crit Care* **4**(4): 293–299

Miyao H, Miyasaka K, Hirokawa T *et al* (1996) Consideration of the international standard for airway humidification using simulated secretions in an artificial airway. *Respir Care* **41**(1): 43–49

Odell A, Allder A, Bayne R *et al* (1993) Endotracheal suction for adult, non-head injured, patients. *A review of the literature, Intensive and Critical Care Nursing* **9**(4): 274–278

Oh T (1988) Ventilation — Matching man, mode and machine. *BrJ Hosp Med* **40**: 216–220

Pappert D, Rossaint R, Slama K *et al* (1994) Influence of positioning on ventilation-perfusion relationships in severe Adult Respiratory Distress Syndrome. *Chest* **106**: 1511–1516

ParkerKP (1995) Promoting sleep and rest in critically ill patients. *Crit Care Clinics North America* **7**(2): 337–349

Pearce J (1994) Communication in critical care nursing. In: Millar B, Burnard P (eds) (1994) *Critical care nursing: caring for the critically ill adult*. Bailliere Tindall, London

Petty T (1995) The 'magic' of succesful weaning from mechanical ventilation in chronic obstructive pulmonary disease. *Crit Care Med* **23**(11): 1799

Ponte J (1990) Indications for mechanical ventilation. *Thorax* **45**: 885-890

Rainbow C (1989) *Monitoring the critically ill patient*. Heinemann Nursing, Oxford

Raymond S (1995) Normal saline installation before suctioning: helpful or harmful? A review of the literature. *Am J Nurs* **4**(4): 267–271

Redick EL (1993) Closed-system, in-line endotracheal suctioning. *Crit Care Nurse* **13**: 47–51

Rivara D, Artucio H, Arcos J *et al* (1984) Positional hypoxaemia during artificial ventilation. *Crit Care Med* **12**(5): 436–438

Richless C (1991) Current trends in mechanical ventilation. *Crit Care Nurse* **11**(3): 41–50

Robb J (1993) An overview of ventilator observations. *Inten Crit Care Nurs* **9**: 201–207

Rudy E, Turner B, Baun M *et al* (1991) Endotracheal suctioning
in adults with head injury. *Heart Lung* **20**(6): 667–674

Ryan DW, Pelosi P (1996) The prone position in acute
respiratory distress syndrome. *Br Med J* **312**: 860–861

Sonnesso G (1991) Are you ready to use pulse oxymetry? *Nurs*
21(8)

Stacy KM (1996) Pulmonary therapeutic management. In: Urden
LA, Lough ME, Stacy KM (eds) *Priorities in Critical Care
Nursing* (2nd edn). Mosby, St Louis

Stillwell SB (1996) *Mosby's Critical care reference* (2nd edition).
Mosby, St Louis.

Tasota F, Wesmiller S (1994) Assessing ABGs maintaining the
delicate balance. *Nurs* **94**: 34–44

Thorens J-B, Kaelin R, Jolliet P (1995) Influence of the quality of
nursing on the duration of weaning from mechanical
ventilation in patients with chronic obstructive pulmonary
disease. *Crit Care Med* **23**: 1807–1815

Tyler ML (1984) The respiratory effects of body positioning and
immobilisation. *Respir Care* **29**(5): 472–483

Warren J, Higenbottam T (1996) Caution with nitric oxide.
Lancet **348**: 629–630

Weilitz PB (1993) Weaning the patient from mechanical
ventilation. *Crit Care Nurse* **13**: 33–41

West J (1990) *Respiratory physiology — the essentials* (4th
edition). Williams and Wilkins, Baltimore

Westcott C (1995) The sedation of patients in intensive care
units: a nursing review. *Inten Crit Care Nurs* **11**(1): 26–31

Woodrow P (1997) Nitric oxide: some nursing implication. *Inten
Crit Care Nurs* **13**(2): 87–92

Vasbinder-Dillon D (1988) Understanding mechanical
ventilation. *Crit Care Nurse* **8**(7): 42–56

Zack M, PontoppidanH, Kazemi H (1974) The effect of lateral
positions on gas exchange in pulmonary disease. *Am Rev
Respir Dis* **110**: 49–55

2

Managing the nursing priorities in the patient requiring haemo-dynamic monitoring

Introduction

The assessment of cardiovascular and pulmonary response to critical illness and therapeutic intervention is an essential element of nursing care in intensive care. The nurse's responsibilities include the ability to collect accurate assessment data, recognise and anticipate deterioration and manage the patients' care accordingly. Skilled assessment and intervention requires an understanding of the pathophysiological changes that may occur.

The aims of this chapter are to:

- describe the functions and clinical uses of the pulmonary artery catheter
- discuss effective strategies of assessing and managing the priorities of nursing care following the insertion of a pulmonary artery catheter (PAC)
- discuss the monitoring and prevention of complications which are associated with insertion of a PAC.

Rationale for use of haemodynamic monitoring

Monitoring haemodynamic parameters enables the critical care team to assess the effects of therapeutic intervention on perfusion and oxygenation of the tissues. For many patients admitted to the critical care environment, physiological parameters such as the heart's rate and rhythm together with oxygen saturation levels can be obtained from non-invasive monitoring of the electrocardiogram (ECG) or using pulse oximetry. Invasive monitoring of arterial and venous pressure, blood gas levels and urine output can also provide a general picture of the patient's haemodynamic status, which is used to direct care and treatment. However, the patient in shock or with deranged pulmonary/cardiac function, may have altered pulmonary or systemic vascular resistance. Its existence is difficult to detect using routine systems of monitoring, therefore management may be inappropriate. Continuous monitoring of blood pressure (MAP), central venous pressure (CVP), heart rate (HR) and urine output together with physical signs and symptoms such as tachypnoea or chest X-ray changes are not sensitive indicators of rapid deterioration in the cardiovascular and pulmonary systems, nor do they provide information on tissue oxygenation or left ventricular function. A lag time may occur, for example blood pressure may not fall for some time after a drop in cardiac output (Darovic, 1995).

Therapy within intensive care areas has become more sophisticated and the management of shock remains an area of research and exploration. As a result, trends in management require a system that provides accurate data and the facilitation of rapid intervention to assist in predicting and preventing further deterioration (Coombs, 1993; Kong and Singer, 1997). The 1970s saw the development of the PAC which enabled a comprehensive calculation of a number of physiological parameters to reflect the patient's haemodynamic status (*Table 2.1*). Calculation of the data generates the 'haemodynamic profile' of the critically ill patient.

The pulmonary artery catheter

The pulmonary artery catheter is made of radio opaque polyvinylchloride. The catheter is 110 cm long, marked in 10 cm increments, is multilumen and for adults the size is 7–8 FG. A balloon, with an inflation volume of 1.5 ml is located at the tip of the catheter. The catheter is usually inserted into the left or right subclavian vein, although this approach is thought to carry a higher risk of pneumothorax (Kong and Singer, 1997). Alternatively, the internal or external jugular vein can be cannulated, however this approach is associated with a greater incidence of line related infection (Mermel and Maki, 1994).

Table 2.1: Parameters measured by pulmonary artery catheter (direct and derived measurement)

Measured
Pulmonary artery pressure — systolic, diastolic and mean (PAP)
Pulmonary capillary wedge pressure (PCWP)
Right atrial temperature (core temperature)
Derived information
Cardiac output (CO)
Cardiac index (CI)
Stroke volume (SV)
Systemic vascular resistance (SVR)
Pulmonary vascular resistance (PVR)
Left and right ventricular stroke work index (LVSWI)
Oxygen delivery (DO_2)
Oxygen consumption (VO_2)
Mixed venous oxygen saturation (SvO_2)

During insertion transitory dysrhythmias may occur as the catheter passes through the heart's chambers into the pulmonary artery causing irritation of the anatomical structures. The assisting nurse should therefore observe the ECG and report rhythm changes. Pressures and waveforms that occur in each location of the catheter as it passes through the right side of the heart, are observed and recorded (*Figure 2.1*). The standard PAC thermodilution catheter contains a number of lumens which open out at different points along the catheter. The functions of each lumen and their termination points are summarised in *Table 2.2*.

Two lumens open out at the tip of the catheter which, once in place, will be located in the pulmonary artery. The distal port can be connected to a pressure transducer and used to measure pulmonary artery pressure (PAP) and pulmonary capillary wedge pressures (PCWP). Drugs and

Figure 2.1: Waveforms and pressures observed following pulmonary artery catheterisation

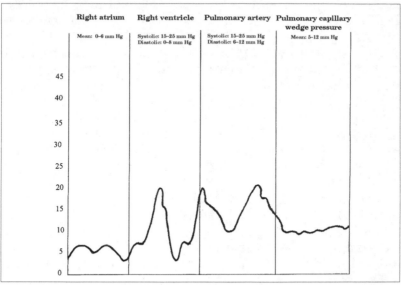

fluids are not usually administered through the distal port as vascular reaction or tissue damage may occur resulting in pulmonary infarction (Darovic, 1995). However, blood can be aspirated from the distal port to monitor mixed venous oxygen saturation (SvO$_2$).

Table 2.2: Summary of parameters measured from various ports

Parameter measured	Measured via	Lumen termination point	Distance from insertion in subclavian or internal jugular
Pulmonary artery pressures	Distal port	tip of catheter	35–40 cm (from right subclavian vein) 40–45 cm (from right jugular vein)
Pulmonary artery temperature	Thermistor port	terminates 4 cm from tip	
Right atrial pressure	Proximal port	terminates in right atrium 30 cm from tip of catheter	15–20 cm
Cardiac output	Proximal injectate port	terminates 31 cm from tip	

The second lumen is connected to the balloon, which is located 1 cm from the tip, this port enables balloon inflation using a syringe. Inflation of the balloon and the flow of blood facilitates the flotation of the catheter into a peripheral pulmonary artery. Occlusion of the peripheral artery, when the balloon is inflated, prevents blood from travelling from the right side of the heart through the pulmonary artery into a small section of the pulmonary bed. At this stage the catheter tip, which is located beyond the balloon, measures the pulmonary capillary wedge pressure (PCWP, normal= 5–12mmHg, *Figure 2.1*), which is a now a reflection of left atrial pressures detected through the pressure in the pulmonary bed and in turn equates with left ventricular end-diastolic pressure (LVEDP) (Hopkinson, 1985).

In practice, PCWP is regarded as an indirect estimate of LVEDP. When the balloon is inflated a 'wedged' trace should be seen displayed on the monitor. Continuous assessment of the patient who has PAC catheter *in situ* should include observation of the waveforms displayed, this is discussed in greater detail further on.

Right atrial pressures can be monitored via the proximal port if connected to a pressure transducer. The proximal infusion lumen terminates 31 cm from the catheter tip. The fourth lumen contains a heat sensitive wire. The lumen terminates at the level of the pulmonary artery, about 4 cm from the catheter tip. The thermistor port can be connected to a cardiac output computer (Darovic, 1995).

Calculation of cardiac output involves the injection of a known volume, usually 5–10 mls, of cold 5% glucose or 0.9% sodium chloride solution into the proximal injectate port which terminates in the right atrium (30 cm from the catheter tip). The solution mixes with pulmonary artery blood and cools it. The time taken for the cooled blood to flow from the exit point in the right atrium to the thermistor is recorded together with the difference in temperature generating a thermodilution curve. The computer then calculates the cardiac output. Usually a mean of three serial recordings is recorded as the cardiac output value (Medley *et al*, 1992).

Table 2.3: Normal values of some haemodynamic parameters that can be measured using a PAC

Normal values		
Pulmonary artery pressure	Systolic	15–25 mmHg
	Diastolic	5–15 mmHg
	Mean	10–20 mmHg
	Wedge	5–12 (mean)
Cardiac output	4–8 litres/min	
Stroke volume	60–130 ml	
Cardiac index	2.5–4.2 litres/min/m^{-2}	
Systemic vascular resistance	900–1600 dyn/sec/cm^{-5}	
Pulmonary vascular resistance	20–120 dyn/sec/cm^{-5}	

Indications for use

Effective assessment and evaluation of the critically ill includes establishing factors that may be impinging on tissue oxygenation. Disease conditions and response to therapy therefore need to be accurately established. The PAC is used to determine the patients haemodynamic status and direct appropriate care.

Table 2.4: Indications for use of a pulmonary artery catheter

General indications for use
• assessment of cartiovascular function and response to treatment
• shock — all types
• assessment of pulmonary status and response to treatment
• assessment of fluid requirements
• assessment of patients undergoing major surgery with a major vascular/organ dysfunction

The nurse's role in caring for a patient is to monitor and document the physiological parameters obtained from the PAC. This information can then be used by the nurse to manage prescribed drug or fluid requirements appropriately. The nurse should therefore be able to recognise changes to the haemodynamic profile which indicate improvement or deterioration. The following tables (*2.5* and *2.6*), list possible parameter alterations that may be seen with a number of patient conditions.

Table 2.5: Examples of affected parameters according to disease processes

Condition	Parameter	Change
Pulmonary		
Oedema	PCWP	increased
ARDS	PA, PVR, PCWP	Increased, low or normal
Embolus and hypertension	PVR, PA, RV, RAP	increased
Cardiac		
LVF	PCWP	increased
Ischaemic heart disease	Stroke vol	low
Cardiac tamponade	Stroke vol	low
Left ventricular infarction	PCWP	increased

In general, the critical nature of an individual's condition will determine the level of derangement of PAC pressures.

Table 2.6: Examples of haemodynamic responses to shock

Condition	Parameter	Change
Sepsis		
vasodilation phase	SVR, CVP, PCWP, CO	decreased increased
vasoconstrictive phase	SVR, PVR	increased
Cardiogenic shock	PCWP, CVP, SVR, CO	all increased decreased
Hypovolaemia	RAP, PAP, PCWP, CO SVR	all decreased increased

While there is increasing evidence that nurses are taking a more proactive role in the manipulation of PACs (Coombs, 1993; Darovic, 1995; Burns *et al*, 1996), concern has been expressed about the level of knowledge that critical care nurses have about the catheters. A study of nurses in the United States revealed a deficit in knowledge that raised concerns about the quality of the PAC data collected and the appropriateness of the following treatment. Burns *et al*, (1996) suggest that educational methods need to be further examined and the setting of quality standards of care to ensure safety of patient care. Certainly, patient outcome is not likely to be improved if the use and understanding of the catheter is poorly addressed.

Current developments in monitoring haemodynamic status

A number of modifications have been made to the standard PAC which can increase the amount and accuracy of available data.

Continuous cardiac output monitoring

Bolus methods of thermodilution to establish cardiac output, provides information on an intermittent basis and relates to a brief point in time. The effects of ventilation are difficult to control and, in addition, the method is subject to user error and is time consuming (Guilbeau and Applegate, 1996; Jakobsen, 1995). Continuous cardiac output monitoring provides 'real time' information that does not require user intervention. The PAC has a thermal filament that is located 14 to 25 cm from the distal tip which produces intermittent heat signals. Heat is transferred to blood at the level of the right atrium, which is then sensed by a thermistor at the tip, located in the pulmonary artery. The resultant temperature change and time taken is used by the computer to plot cardiac output (Guilbeau and Applegate, 1996). Jakobsen (1995) argues that not only is this method of monitoring more accurate it can also give an early warning of spontaneous wedge position, thereby assisting the nurse in detecting potential complications.

Fibreoptic mixed venous oxygen saturation monitoring

Tissue oxygenation requires an adequate cardiac output. However, measuring cardiac output alone does not identify the reasons why cardiac output is altered. Parameters that contribute to changes in cardiac output need to be identified and managed. One such parameter is that of mixed venous oxygen saturation (SvO^2). In health this value is about 75%. A fall in SvO^2 indicates that the patient is attempting to preserve oxygen balance in response to an increased oxygen demand or reduced supply (Jakobsen, 1995). SvO^2 can be calculated by taking intermittent blood samples from the PAC. More recently though the incorporation of fibreoptics within the PAC allows continuous monitoring of SvO^2. Continuous assessment will enable the nurse or doctor to evaluate more rapidly the response to therapy and provide an early indicator of problems in oxygen delivery (Hayden, 1993).

Transoesophageal doppler ultrasound

The transoesophageal doppler ultrasound is a non invasive method of measuring haemodynamic parameters. An oesophageal probe is inserted through the mouth into the oesophagus where it measures sound waves generated by blood descending through the thoracic aorta. A visual display of the waveform is generated and used to calculate stroke volume, left ventricular filling and contractility. Derived measurements of cardiac output and volume status contribute to the provision of a haemodynamic profile. The main advantage of this technique is that it is non-invasive, simple to use and safe (Higgins and Singer, 1993). Higgins and Singer also point out that the delay in inserting a PAC because of the high costs or lack of appropriate equipment, lack of expertise, and concerns about the risk-benefit ratio, could be avoided by using the transoesophageal doppler ultrasound. As a result, intervention can be initiated early and organ failure perhaps prevented.

Limitations on the use of pulmonary artery catheters

The PAC is widely used within intensive care areas to monitor haemodynamic function. However, it is an invasive form of monitoring, therefore patients are more likely to develop a line related sepsis. In addition manipulation of the catheter may cause perforation of the heart wall or great vessels. Nevertheless it is argued that catheterisation assists in effective diagnosis and improved management (Connors, *et al*, 1990; Mimoz *et al*, 1994; Shoemaker *et al*, 1988). Robin (1985) however, has questioned the continued use and value of flotation catheters and suggested that there was a cult of abuse. His predictions have been validated as problems with the poor utilisation of data and its lack of impact on the management of care (Mimoz *et al*, 1994; Steingrub *et al*, 1991; Richardson and Reddy, 1994) has led some to further argue that the benefits do not outweigh the risks (Steingrub, 1993). More recent studies support this and have reported that the catheter is associated with increased costs and length of intensive care/hospital stay and importantly, an increased incidence in mortality (Gore *et al*, 1987;Connors *et al*, 1996). Not surprisingly, demands for re-evaluation of the PAC have been proposed, this also includes training of intensive care personnel in the analysis of data and subsequent management responses. Moreover, Nightingale (1993) and Steingrub (1993) emphasise that not all ITU patients should undergo pulmonary catheterisation, strict clinical criteria as well as a risk and benefit analysis should be applied when making decisions about the need for PA catheter insertion.

Table 2.7: Priorities of care for the patient with PAC

Nursing priority	Intervention/management
Optimising accuracy of PAC readings	• monitor and document patient position • evaluate the effect of respiratory variations • evaluate the impact of altered physiology on clinical data • consistency with thermo-dilution techniques
Assessment and interpretation of changes in PA	• monitoring of PA wave form • manipulation of PAC

Maintenance of PA catheter and patient safety	• maintaining patency of PAC and monitoring for alterations in waveforms • maintaining asepsis of system
Monitoring complications	• assessing for and preventing infection • assessing for and preventing rhythm disturbances • assessing for and preventing PA perforation and balloon rupture • assessing for and preventing pulmonary infarction • assessing for and preventing catheter knotting

Optimising accuracy of PAC readings

As emphasised earlier, one of the strengths of having a PAC in place is to assist in determining the patient's current clinical status and so enable more exacting decisions about treatment. This, however, depends on the accuracy of the readings and the skill of clinicians at extracting the significance of the data. There are a number of known physiological and technical factors which can affect the interpretation of haemodynamic measurements, and arguably a nurse at the bedside in ITU/CCU must be aware of how each of these variables may influence patient data.

Patient position

Traditionally patients are often placed in the supine position to standardise the precision of haemodynamic measurements. It may be thought to be detrimental to the well being of some patients to lie them in this way, such as those with a head or spinal injury or with acute pulmonary disorders. In addition repeated backrest changes may interrupt the quality of rest and sleep patterns as well as induce unnecessary pain and discomfort (Darovic, 1995). Nevertheless reliable haemodynamic measurements can be obtained in a variety of postures but, to guarantee accuracy the selected position must be used throughout, measuring techniques must be standardised, and each patient should be assessed individually.

The discrepancy that exists in haemodynamic readings between the supine and backrest elevated position can be attributed to the forces of gravity as these give rise to differences in central venous return, with a net effect that these are reduced in the latter. However, the clinical appearance of the patient may not always correlate with this. Darovic (1995) and Wilkinson (1992) recommend that when reviewing the information, it is the overall trend over time that should be considered because this is a more valid indicator of progress rather than a single measure, as the measures may be influenced by a range of factors. Moreover, when making judgements about pressure data, the position at which the recordings were made must be documented in the care plan and patient flow sheet.

To assure accurate readings, data from supine or backrest elevated positions must not be compared to the lateral postures, as the reference level for PA pressure measurement can produce wide variations in readings relative to the standard positions (Bridges and Woods, 1993; Schermer, 1988). In addition, the following points below must be employed on every occassion:

i) The transducer must be placed at the same level/point on the patients chest prior to each evaluation.

ii) The phlebostatic axis (ie. the intersection of the fourth intercostal space lateral to the thorax and midaxillary line) has been validated as the key reference point for acquiring accurate PAC measurements and thus contributes to the accuracy and reliability of the data. The level of the left atrium can also be employed as a standard reference point, but this must be used consistently when obtaining haemodynamic measures.

iii) The transducer may require regular calibration and zeroing depending on the technology available (and local policies).

Effects of respiratory variations

With spontaneous respiration, the intrathoracic pleural pressures decrease during inspiration and increase during expiration. The reverse occurs during positive pressure ventilation (West, 1990). This increase in intra-alveolar and pleural pressures that ensues during the inspiratory phase of mechanical ventilation (MV) is conveyed to the cardiac vasculature resulting in changes to both PA and PCWP measures (Booker and Arnold, 1993; Bridges and Woods, 1993). Similarly, if the application of positive end-expiratory pressure (PEEP) is greater than 10cm H_2O, not only does this increase the level of intrathoracic pressure but the readings will not reflect the actual haemodynamic status as the relationship between PCWP and left atrial pressures is widened. It is also possible that if the catheter is in a pulmonary vessel which is situated in a lung zone above the left atrium, the disparity between readings increases particularly as PEEP can produce a higher alveolar to capillary pressure gradient. Accordingly, it is important to check the X-ray and ensure that the tip of the catheter is equal to or below the left atrium (Schermer, 1988; Bridges and Woods, 1993). Cathelyn (1997), also advises that nurses should assess for evidence of the depth of respiratory movements as these cause pressure waves to oscillate and portray abnormal values that may misguide decisions.

Guaranteeing the validity of PAC measures relies on the use of exacting methods. A variety of techniques for improving the validity of haemodynamic measures have been proposed, including the temporary disconnection of the ventilator, applying breath-hold or recording the mean pressure from the digital display. However, some of these approaches may adversely affect the patient's condition and do not produce consistent values. In contrast, reliable data can be obtained at the end of expiration as, at this stage of the respiratory cycle, both intrathoracic and atmospheric pressures tend to be equal. This in turn provides a credible baseline for further measures and is a technique that is supported by extensive research (Cathelyn, 1997; Darovic, 1995; Johnson and Schumann, 1995; Levine-Silverman and Johnson, 1990).

During artificial ventilation PA and PCWP waves have altered values when compared to those recorded during spontaneous ventilation. Moreover, in the ventilated patient the PA and PCWP waveforms rise with inspiration and will dip downwards during expiration, whereas in spontaneous breathing the individual waveform decreases in inspiration and is followed by a rise during the phase of expiration (Levine-Silverman and Johnson, 1990). Awareness of this difference when reviewing a printed trace can assist the critical care nurse to interpret changes in the patient accurately and to discern the validity of the data.

This is in contrast to relying on visual numerical displays as their reliability as the basis for judgements has been widely questioned (Bridges and Woods, 1993; Johnson and Schumann, 1995; Pierpont, 1987). Pierpoint (1987) comments that most monitoring systems produce calculated visual read-outs that are based on the highest, lowest and mean values over a span of time, but omit to include changes in respiratory cycle. The concern is that the indiscriminate choice and averaging of digital readings tends to be blindly accepted even though they do not accurately express the patient's status and as a result lead to erroneous actions. Levine-Silverman and Johnson (1990) in a small study of patients admitted to critical units noted differences between graph and digital measurements and recommended that the latter be regularly compared with the former in order to avoid instituting incorrect therapies. More recently, Johnson and Schumann (1995) compared three methods of measuring haemodynamic data in critically ill patients during a period of MV and during spontaneous breathing. To assess the merits between recording techniques they compared graphic recordings of haemodynamic waveforms with digital bedside displays. Their findings revealed that the use of graphic readings provided a reliable measurement of haemodynamic pressures at end-expiration when contrasted to numerical displays. However, Booker and Arnold (1993) add that with tachypnoeic, erratic breathing patterns and mechanically ventilated patients reading the end-expiration phase is more difficult.

Confidence with assessing patient data may be increased by either displaying waveforms against a calibrated scale, by obtaining a printed trace or by freezing the screen and analysing the waves, but always taking into account respiratory fluctuations. Cathelyn (1997) also recommends that the assessment is documented and repeated according to local protocols as increasingly nurses are expected to titrate fluids or medications in response to clinical data, and thus, their actions carry implications for the patient.

Altered physiology

There are many clinical conditions, previously mentioned, that make the assessment and interpretation of haemo- dynamic measures complex or which can mislead clinicians. For example, mitral regurgitation, left ventricular dysfunction, hyperdynamic heart, and mitral stenosis can all produce readings that either do not correlate with either standard PCWP and left ventricular end diastolic pressure or which can cause artifact or waveform damping (Darovic, 1995).

Medications can also influence haemodynamic measurements and the continued evaluation of parameters provides direct evidence of therapeutic effectiveness. For example, nitrates used in cardiogenic shock will decrease systemic vascular resistance as well as preload, thus contributing to myocardial performance. Similarly, inhaled nitric oxide can be prescribed to decrease pulmonary hypertension and pulmonary vascular resistance in order to augment gas exchange. Whereas the administration of dobutamine and noradrenaline in the case of septacaemic shock can be employed to increase systemic vascular resistance and myocardial contractility with the aim of improving cardiac output. In contrast, a sudden drop in PCWP may occur in response to the administration of diuretics, but should rise following an infusion of plasma.

Consistency with thermodilution techniques

As stated before this requires the injection of a known volume at a known temperature through the proximal port of the PAC. A number of elements such as catheter place- ment, the patient's condition, technical aspects and operator technique may all bias the quality and accuracy of the measurements (Darovic, 1995; Schermer, 1988). As mentioned earlier, the respiratory cycle is a significant variable related to cardiac output studies. It is imperative that the frequency of measurements is justified and that personnel are experienced and trained in the rigour of the procedures as well as in appraising the data.

Assessment and interpretation of changes in PA

Monitoring PA waveform

During the time that the right sided catheter is in place and when not 'wedging' the balloon, it is standard practice to have the PA waveform on continuous visual display. There are a number of reasons for this and familiarity with normal values and with the shape of the curves is crucial for rapidly discerning whether adverse changes have occurred.

The PA waveform provides a baseline for locating its position and highlighting potential problems. The implication of forward displacement or of failing to deflate the balloon, is the possible occlusion of a capillary resulting in pulmonary infarction which is manifest by the sudden but distinct change in waveform shape. Conversely, backward migration, caused by accidental pulling, may result in the PAC lying in the right ventricle and thus the readings will not be helpful. A chest X-ray is desirable in these circumstances. In addition, a record of the external catheter length should be made at the beginning of every shift (to nearest 10 cm), as this serves as a marker from which to make an evaluation as to whether there has been displacement from PA position.

The PA trace also reinforces that the balloon has not been left 'wedged' as both the graph and digital display differ from PCW pressures and wave contours. The wave should also be seen to fluctuate with the respiratory cycle, and the dicrotic notch should be visible.

Figure 2.2: PA waveform

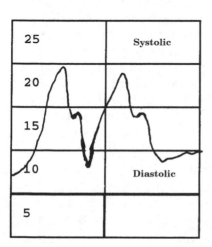

Manipulation of PAC

Stokes and Jowett (1985) emphasise that the care of the patient must always encompass, physiological, psychological and haemodynamic parameters. They add that nurses should also have responsibility for calibration, recording pressures and catheter related problems. To achieve this, an understanding of patient pathology, waveforms, pressures and the effects of various interventions will assist the nurse in being able to rapidly recognise and anticipate changes and institute an appropriate plan of care. Hagland and Wilkinson (1993) suggest that in the past, wedging the balloon and determining cardiac output using a flotation catheter were considered extended nursing roles. Whereas Wilkinson (1992) has stated that central to the nurses' function is the assessment, monitoring, titration and implementation of nursing strategies based on the knowledge and expertise of practitioners. Clearly there is some broad consensus, although this needs to be specified further. Although Hagland and Wilkinson (1993) refer to the Scope of Professional Practice (1992) and advance that this should enable nurses to perform specified tasks only when they can demonstrate competence.

Biel and Stotts (1995) conducted a study to examine what was expected of nurses with regard to handling the PAC. It was reported that only a third of their sample of 503 critical care nurses were allowed to manipulate or withdraw the PA catheter back into the right atrium, and just under half could remove the invasive line. It is however claimed that the risk of complications have been low with regard to the manipulation of a PA catheter when nurses are provided with a comprehensive training package prior to undertaking the role. Additionally, the establishment of strict guidelines and practice protocols was instrumental in achieving this outcome. Despite this, the manipulation of PA catheters by nurses appears not to be widely practised. Earlier, in one study which examined the complications associated with 205 catheter removals by nurses who had been prepared in this role, it was noted that 10 patients experienced brief rhythm disturbances which required no treatment. In one individual whose PAC had been in place for 10 days, there was initial resistance during withdrawal and this was succesfully removed without incident (Roundtree, 1991).

Maintenance of PA catheter and patient safety

Maintaining catheter function seems to be a major nursing role and can be broken into line patency and waveform interpretation (Baas, 1996). With regards to patency, regular checks must include ensuring that the flush system is delivering 3mls/hour of heparinised saline and that the pressure bag should be set at 300mmHg. While it may be reasonable to regularly perform a short (1–2 secs) manual flush to ensure that the line does not obstruct, nurses should avoid delivering longer purges. This is because if a clot has formed at the catheter tip, it may become dislodged and be transported elsewhere (under a pressure of 300mmHg) resulting in dire consequences for the patient.

To begin to interpret abnormal waveforms, one has to consider the causes for this. A flattened/dampened trace for example, suggests that there are air bubbles in the infusion system and these need to be flushed out without entering the patient. However, this wave pattern may also occur if the catheter tip is adjacent to the wall of the pulmonary artery, in this instance the balloon should be inflated and placed slightly forward. Other explanations for a wave damping are if the catheter is obstructed or if it is kinked.

By comparison, evidence of a low amplitude trace suggests that blood has backtracked into the transducer but, more commonly, it is associated with loose connections and low pressure in the infusion bag. However, if the waveform unexpectedly changes, this implies either forward or backward migration into a pulmonary artery or right ventricle, respectively. In the case of the catheter accidentally wedging, the conscious patient should be asked to cough as this may assist in dislodging it from its position. In the event that this is unsuccessful, medical assistance should be sought. Often a sudden wave form change, simply requires calibration of the transducer and rezeroing (Rainbow, 1989). Troubleshooting thus relies on a systematic and structured examination of the visible length of the PAC, the transducer, dome, connections and flush system to enable the bedside nurse to identify the problems. A comprehensive assessment must include a review of chest X-rays starting with the date the PAC was inserted.

Monitoring for complications

The complications resulting from PA catheterisation are many and are associated with insertion, advancement and removal. This section deals with the most often experienced.

Assessing for and preventing infections

Before introducing a pulmonary artery catheter, the decision should be weighed carefully as most critically ill patients will be immunocompromised and so at risk from local and generalised infections. Factors such as age, severity of underlying disease, and nutritional status may influence the incidence of infection rates. Apart from maintaining meticulous asepsis at all times and regular temperature monitoring for signs of infection, a clear dressing at the puncture site will allow inspection of the wound for evidence of oozing and local inflammation (Masters, 1989; Wadas, 1994). Although the incidence of infection can occur with central lines, this is more likely to occur in those with an internal jugular line (Mermel and Maki,1994). Where there is suspicion of infection, blood cultures should be taken and antibiotics commenced. In some institutions the PAC is removed when there is clinical evidence of infection, the catheter tip is then cut and sent for microbiology.

Changing of infusion lines, tubing and flush solution is an area where contamination can occur. Chulay (1995) has recently advised that frequent replacement of invasive systems is not supported by research. Indeed, one study reported that the risk of contamination increases as a result of regular disconnection of monitoring systems and the authors also suggested that invasive systems may need changing once a week (O'Malley *et al*, 1994). Although in many units PAC are routinely removed after 48 hours.

Assessing for and preventing cardiac dysrhythmias

Rhythm disturbances are a common complication and will typically occur during the passage of the PAC across the chambers, when manipulating the device and during removal. Ventricular ectopics or salvo's of ventricular tachycardia may be observed on the ECG monitor and are caused by mechanical irritation of the valves and endocardial surface. Right bundle branch block is also a potential problem and in those with left bundle branch block the incidence of complete heart block is high (Darovic, 1995). It is sensible that prior to insertion, manipulation or complete withdrawal, a review of serum electrolytes and cardiac enzymes is performed as any derangements may precipitate sustained life-threatening dysrhythmias. Resuscitation equipment should always be at hand during these manoeuvres and the patient should have their ECG monitored (Darovic, 1995; Masters, 1989; Wadas, 1994).

Assessing for and preventing PA perforation and balloon rupture

Pulmonary capillary perforation can happen as a result of rapid balloon inflation, hyperinflation or repeated balloon wedging, activities that may also result in rupture of the balloon. Failing to inflate the balloon while advancing the catheter, spontaneous migration of catheter, and aggressive manipulation are other causes. According to Masters (1989) and Wadas (1994), patients most at risk are those receiving anticoagulant therapy, those who are suffering from pulmonary hypertension and those with hypothermia as this leads to catheter stiffening and thus raising the incidence of trauma. Evidence of sudden haemoptysis should raise immediate suspicions and should be reported immediately, as a haemothorax, respiratory distress or full cardiac arrest may also occur unless the haemorrhaging is stopped.

In contrast, balloon rupture occurs because over time the thin latex of the balloon begins to loose elasticity and is also weakened by the absorption of lipoproteins from the circulation. In addition, if the rate of inflations exceeds 70, the balloon life expectancy is reduced (Darovic, 1995). The main indicators of balloon puncture is a lack of resistance during inflation, failure to wedge and when the syringe plunger does not spring back after inflation. In this situation, the PAC should be removed and replaced if necessary. It is important not to exceed the recommended air volume during inflation and to keep balloon inflations to a minimum. Charting how often PCWP readings are obtained may be useful in guiding patient care.

Assessing for and preventing pulmonary infarction

The causes of this complication include prolonged balloon occlusion and thrombus formation at the tip of the catheter. Patients with low cardiac output and high haematocrit are most under threat risk. Equally, the PAC may migrate forward under the influence of blood flow and spontaneously wedge in the lumen of a small vessel. If the balloon has not been deflated properly or if it has been accidentally inflated, this too can lead to pulmonary infarction. The patient may thus complain of chest pain or shortness of breath. Also, the respiratory rate may increase, blood pressure and oxygen saturations fall, and haemoptysis may be evident on coughing or when performing endothracheal suctioning if MV.

It is vital that when wedging the balloon, that this should be kept inflated for not longer than 15 seconds and that the heparinised saline flush system is maintained to prevent clot formation. If a repeat PCWP is necessary, a short interval should pass before obtaining a second set of readings. As stated before, once the balloon has been deflated, the nurse must assess the PA waveform on the screen as this will confirm catheter placement and serve as a reference point for gauging possible migration. Nurses must also be able to detect unexpected dampened or wedged patterns and act accordingly.

Assessing for and preventing catheter knotting

Knotting can occur during placement or removal of the PAC and can lead to valvular and vessel damage particularly if it loops or coils form, which then knot around mitral and pulmonary structures. Patients prone to catheter knotting are those with a temporary or permanent pacemaker, and who have a dilated right ventricle but a small bore PAC. Also those with an excessive catheter length or with high pulmonary pressures are also at risk (Masters, 1989; Wadas, 1994). As there are no presenting symptoms, regular assessment of the chest X-ray is vital, and if resistance is encountered during withdrawal stages or during manipulation this requires radiological investigation.

Practical suggestions to prevent complications should begin with an analysis of catheter length, as mentioned before there should not be more than 5 markings on the catheter (15cms from right atrium to pulmonary artery, and 25-from neck point to right atrium). Advancing the catheter should be avoided in the absence of recognisable waveforms as this suggests coiling or even knotting. If unsure, referring to X-ray is mandatory, Wadas (1994) also indicates that catheter removal in the presence of a pacemaker is contraindicated for nurses working in the United States. In exceptional cases surgical intervention may be necessary to remove the catheter but it may be unknotted under fluoroscopy.

While the complications mentioned in this chapter occur infrequently and have been reduced with more sophisticated technology (Guilbeau and Applegate, 1996; Jakobsen, 1995), the increased use of right sided catheters for diagnostic purposes and as a valuable adjunct for the management of critically ill patients, suggests that nurses must remain vigilant. Moreover, as nurses become more responsible for a range of tasks previously undertaken by physicians, their acceptance must always be governed by serving the needs of the patient, improving quality and safety of care. It is unequivocal that for nurses to be able to accurately identify, interpret changes and evaluate the significance of haemodynamic measurements, they should possess wide knowledge and expertise of pathophysiological and pharmacological influences on patient parameters. They must also be conversant with catheter operations and their maintenance, and be able to institute appropriate strategies that prevent and correct changes in clinical status.

References

Baas L (1996) Care of the cardiac patient. In: Kinney M, Packa DR (eds) *Andreoli's comprehensive cardiac care*. Mosby, St Louis, Baltimore: chap 8

Biel MH, Stotts J (1995) The RN's role in the manipulation of pulmonary artery catheters. *Crit Care Nurse* **15**(1): 30–35

BookerKJ Arnold JS (1993) Respiratory induced changes on the pulmonary capillary wedge pressure tracing. *Crit Care Nurse* **13**(3): 80–88

Bridges EJ, Woods SL (1993) Pulmonary artery pressure measurement: state of the art. *Heart Lung* **22**(2): 99–111

Burns D, Burns D, Shively M (1996) Critical Care Nurse's Knowledge of Pulmonary Artery Catheters. *Am J Crit Care* **5**(1): 49–54

Cathelyn J (1997) Avoiding respiratory excursions: obtaining reliable pulmonary capillary wedge pressures. *Dimensions Crit Care Nurs* **16**(1): 2–7

Chulay M (1995) Ask the experts. *Crit Care Nurse* **15**: 108

Connors AF, Speroff T, Dawson NV *et al* (1996) The effectiveness of right hear catheterization in the initial care of critically ill patients. *JAMA* **276**(11): 889–897

Connors AF, Dawson NV, Shaw PK *et al* (1990) Haemodynamic status in critically ill patients with and without acute heart disease. *Chest* **98**: 1200–1206

Coombs M (1993) Haemodynamic profiles and the critical care nurse. *Intensive Crit Care Nurs* **9**: 11–16

Darovic GO (1995) *Haemodynamic Monitoring: Invasive and noninvasive clinical application*. 2nd edition. WB Saunders Co, Philadelphia: chaps 10–11

Gore JM, Goldberg RJ, Spodick DH (1987) A community wide assessment of the use of pulmonary catheters in patients with acute myocardial infarction. *Chest* **92**(4): 721–727

Guilbeau J, Applegate AR (1996) Thermodilution: An advanced technique for measuring continuous cardiac output. *Dimensions Crit Care Nurs* **15**(1): 25–30

Hagland M, Wilkinson B (1993) Making sense of Swan-Ganz monitoring. *Nurs Times* **89**(40): 26–28

Hayden RA (1993) Trend-spotting with an SvO$_2$ monitor. *Am J Nurs* **93**(1): 26–36

Higgins DJ, Singer M (1993) Transoesophageal Doppler for continuous haemodynamic monitoring. *Br J Intensive Care* **3**: 376–378

Hopkinson R (1985) Using pulmonary artery catheters. *Care Crit Ill* **1**(7): 15–20

Jakobsen C-J (1995) Invasive cardiac output monitoring. *Int J Intensive Care* **2**(2): 48–54

Johnson M, Schumann L (1995) Comparison of three methods of measurement of pulmonary artery catheter readings in critically ill patients. *Am J Crit Care* **4**(4): 300–307

Kong R, Singer M (1997) Insertion of a pulmonary artery flotation catheter: how to do it. *Br J Hosp Med* **57**(9): 432–435

Levine-Silverman S, Johnson J (1990) Pulmonary artery pressure measurements. *West J Nurs Res* **12**(4): 488–496

Masters S (1989) Complications of pulmonary artery catheters. *Crit Care Nurse* **9**(9): 82–91

MedleyRS, Delapp TD, Fisher DG (1992) Comparability of the thermodilution cardiac output method: Proximal injectate versus proximal infusion lumens. *Heart Lung* **21**(1): 12–17

Mermel L, Maki D (1994) Infections complications of Swan-Ganz pulmonary artery catheters. *Am J Respir Care Med* **149**: 1020–1036

Mimoz O, Rauss A, Rekik N *et al* (1994) Pulmonary artery catheterization in critically ill patients: A prospective analysis of outcome changes associated with catheter-prompted changes in therapy. *Crit Care Med* **22**(4): 573–579

Nightingale P (1993) The pros and cons of the pulmonary artery catheter. *Care Crit Ill* **9**(3): 104–106

O'Malley MK, Rhame F, Cerra F *et al* (1994) Value of routine pressure monitoring system changes after 72 hours of continuous use. *Crit Care Med* **22**: 1424–1430

Pierpoint GL (1987) Pitfalls of computer use in acute care medicine. *Heart Lung* **16**(2): 207–210

Rainbow C (1989) *Monitoring the critically ill patient.* Heinemann Nursing, London: chap 6

Richardson MS, Reddy V (1994) Use of the pulmonary catheter (Swan-Ganz) catheter in critical care. *Chest* **105**(2): 643

Robin E (1985) The cult of the Swan-Ganz catheter: overuse and abuse of pulmonary flow catheters. *Annals Intern Med* **103**: 445–449

Roundtree WD (1991) Removal of pulmonary artery catheters by registered nurses: a study in safety and complications. *Focus Crit Care* **18**(4): 313–314, 316–318

Schermer L (1988) Physiologic and technical variables affecting haemodynamic measurements. *Crit Care Nurse* **8**(2): 33–40

Shoemaker WC, Appel PL, Kram HB *et al* (1988) Prospective trial 1186 of supernormal values of survivors as therapeutic goals in high-risk surgical patients. *Chest* **94**: 1176–1186

Steingrub JS, Celoria G, Vickers-Lahti M *et al* (1991) Therapeutic impact of pulmonary artery catheterization in a medical/surgical ICU. *Chest* **99**(6): 1451–1455

Steingrub JS (1993) Efficancy of pulmonary artey catherization: fact or fancy. *Med Care Int* April: 25–29

Stokes P, Jowett N (1985) Haemodynamic monitoring with a Swan-Ganz catheter. *Inten Care Nurs* **1**: 3–12

United Kingdom Central Council (1992) *The Scope of Professional Practice.* (UKCC), London

Wadas TM (1994) Pulmonary artery catheter removal. *Crit Care Nurse* **14**: 62–72

West J (1990) *Respiratory physiology — the essentials* (4th edn). Williams and Wilkins, Baltimore

Wilkinson R(1992) Pulmonary artery pressure monitoring. *Nurs Standard* **6**(42): 25–28

3

Managing the nursing priorities in the patient with acute renal failure

The aim of this chapter is to discuss the management and priorities of care for patients who have developed acute renal failure (ARF) and undergoing haemofiltration in an intensive care unit (ITU).

Objectives of this chapter:

- to review the causes, outcome and prognosis of patients who develop acute renal failure and are managed in the ITU
- to identify and analyse the priorities of nursing care and discuss these in the context of the management of the patient
- to outline the current use of continuous renal replacement therapies (CRRT) and discuss the associated nursing care issues.

Acute renal failure is a syndrome, often reversible, that is generally characterised by **a sudden reduction** in kidney function, resulting in the retention of nitrogenous wastes and should be suspected if there is a significant rise in serum urea (>7mmols/litre) and serum creatinine (140mmols/L) with or without oliguria (urine output <400ml/24hours or 0.5ml/kg/hr) (Hulman and Wolfson, 1993; Thadhani et al, 1996). Other key features of ARF will include, electrolyte disturbances, acid-base imbalance, a failure to maintain fluid homeostasis, haemodynamic instability and weight gain (Price, 1994). However, due to the complexity of the disease process, there is still a lack of consensus over the criteria as to what constitutes or accurately defines ARF (Thadhani et al, 1996).

Price (1994), estimates that patients with ARF comprise approximately 10–20% of all those treated in ITU. Bellomo and Noyce (1993a) predict that the number of cases

requiring acute renal support will increase due to technological advances, the expansion of health care knowledge and
the use of complex aggressive therapies performed on the
ageing population who may be suffering with other problems
such as sepsis or chronic conditions. This in turn is likely to
lead to lengthy hospitalisation and increase the costs of
treatment. Further, the rise in complicated surgical
procedures and the wide use of invasive medical technology
means that more patients are being treated who in the past
would not been considered suitable (Bellomo and Noyce,
1993a) this inevitably has impact on outcomes of care and on
prognosis.

Currently, the statistics on mortalities of ARF
illustrate that in the United Kingdom (UK) and abroad these
remain poor and unchanged, ranging between 45–80%
(Chertow *et al*, 1997; Druml, 1996; Liaño *et al*, 1989; Stevens
and Rainford, 1992; Woodrow and Turney, 1992). Although
survival across different patient sub-groups varies, it is the
number of organs which fail that is a significant predictor.

Because of these poor outcomes, studies identifying
the prognosis have in recent years attracted much attention
(Druml, 1996; Brivet *et al*, 1996). In a review of 20 years
experience Druml identified a list of factors that influence
the outcome:

- cause of ARF, (whether the insult is a primary or
  secondary event and whether there are other
  dysfunctional organs)
- whether ARF develops in the ITU setting, rather than
  in the hospital or in the community
- severity of renal injury and need for renal replacement
  therapy
- severity of underlying disorder (the presence of other
  acute illnesses such acute cardiac, infective, or
  respiratory disease)
- co-existing chronic disease (plus age, gender, evidence
  of diabetes, hypertension, hepatic or heart failure)
- treatment variables, (namely whether the patient
  requires inotropic support and total parenteral
  nutrition).

Brivet *et al*, (1996) in a multi-centre study of ITUs identified
similar trends but, in addition, noted that a history of

chronic illness, hospitalisation prior to ITU admission, sepsis, oliguria, and severity of illness (as assessed by APACHE II scoring) were all predictive of a poor prognosis. Whereas Liaño *et al*'s (1989) multivariate analysis revealed that persistent hypotension, deep neurological coma and the need for assisted ventilation have a significant bearing on mortality. As nurses have a primary responsibility for assessing prioritising and initiating interventions that may reduce or avert patient problems, they may influence morbidity and mortality rates related to ARF, thus it has been advanced that their clinical expertise is indispensable (Price, 1994; Stark, 1994).

Causes of acute renal failure and identification of patient problems

Classification of renal failure

Acute renal failure is typically classified into three groups, prerenal, renal and post renal, each is distinguished by the causative factors and the degree of structural damage within the nephron.

Pre-renal

This is any factor that leads to a sudden reduction in perfusion to the kidneys without causing tubular or cellular injury. It is normally the result of a reduced circulating volume and the condition is immediately reversible through correction of the circulatory deficit. It is the most frequent explanation for a rising urea and creatinine as well as for a reduced urine output. The causes of prerenal dysfunction may include burns, dehydration, haemorhage, fever, diuretics, septic shock or severe vomiting and diarrhoea. In one recent study of 20 intensive care units, 17% of patients met the above description (Brivet *et al*, 1996). Generally the kidney's ability to filter, secrete and excrete will remain intact. Moreover, a ratio of urine urea to blood urea of greater that >10 indicates good renal function.

Renal

Here alterations in renal function are associated with structural damage to the tubules and surrounding tissues, and will develop despite correcting the precipitating factors. This form of renal failure may be due either to an ischaemic/prerenal event or to a toxic insult. As the tubules are the main structures involved this gives rise to the term acute tubular necrosis (ATN).

Ischaemic injury results from a sustained drop in circulation, particularly when mean arterial pressure drops below 60mmHg. When this happens, autoregulatory effects are stimulated, namely there is a of release of renin-angiotensin and sympathetic activity. The consequence of this is that the afferent arterioles constrict, glomerular hydrostatic presure falls and therefore the glomerular filtration rate (GFR) is either reduced or ceases (Baer and Lancaster, 1992). Because of these ischaemic changes, the proximal tubule's capacity for sodium reabsorption will be diminished so that the fluid excreted tends to be diluted, high in sodium content but low in volume. The effect of increased level of sodium at the distal tubules, induces a tubuloglomerular feedback mechanism to be activated whose role in health is to vasoconstrict the afferent arteriole and raise mean arterial pressure. However, in the scenario of ATN, glomerular blood flow and filtration pressure falls, and the GFR is compromised further.

More significantly, persistent hypoxia of the renal cells and subsequent metabolic alterations will reduce reserves of adenosine triphosphatase (ATP) disrupting the sodium-potassium pump. The net outcome of this is a shift of sodium and chloride into the cells, whereas potassium, magnesium and inorganic phosphates will be displaced to the extracellular space. This rise in intracellular sodium will be followed by the movement of water into the cells causing swelling which under increased pressure will begin to necrose. Ischaemic cell injury will be equally intensified by a rise of intracellular calcium and by the presence of oxygen free radicals (New and Barton, 1996; Thadhani *et al*, 1996).

With the advent of cell death tubular membrane function will be altered. In addition, casts and necrotic debris will begin to be shed into the lumen causing tubular obstruction. If the blockage of the tubule is complete, back pressure upstream will give rise to a higher intratubular and capsular pressure which in time will exceed arterial hydrostatic pressure and so reduce the potential for filtrate production. Further, as the tubular membrane is damaged it becomes more permeable and with rising pressure it allows the waste products to leak across the insterstitum and into adjacent peritubular capillaries. Not only does back leakage reduce the volume of fluid reaching the collecting ducts, but the filtrate will be reabsorbed into the capillary network and thus into the circulation. According to Norris (1989), the backleak phenomenom accounts for the rapid rise in urea associated with ATN. Other findings of ischaemic ATN include, oliguria, a low urine urea, decreased creatinine clearance, high urinary sodium and an inability to concentrate urine (normal; osmolality is >500 mOsm/kg:ATN it is <300 mOsm/kg, Leaker, 1988; Toto, 1992).

Toxic injury in contrast, is the result of an insult on tubular cells either from nephrotoxic medications, such as cephalosporins or radiographic contrast dye, waste products of septacaemia or endogenous toxins. Much of the pathophysiology is similar to post-ischaemic ATN, however here the basement membrane is spared therefore the recovery is rapid and often the patient may present without oliguria (Baer and Lancaster, 1992; Norris, 1989).

Hulman and Wolfson (1993) also identify glomerulovascular conditions and these are primary vascultic processes such as poliarteritis nodosa, Henoch-Schölein purpura, Goodpastures syndrome, and embolic insults. With glomerulonephritis, antigens stimulate the formation of complexes which on reaching the vascular bed of the kidney become lodged in the basement membrane causing injury and inflamation. This loss of wall at the interface with the capillaries, allows red blood cells and proteins to permeate into the filtrate and thus are found in the urine.

When measuring urine output, nurses must examine for the presence of cellular debris, granular casts and red cells as this provides a useful guide in descriminating whether the patient is in the pre-renal stage or in ATN, especially when there is a reduced volume. A low specific gravity (normal 1.010–1.030), with dilute urine indicates tubular damage, suggestive of ATN. The screening of urine, monitoring for discolouration and for evidence of sediment is vital in alerting to ATN.

Post-renal

Post-renal causes by comparison are associated with an obstruction to the flow of urine. Normally, this may be due to renal calculi, urethral strictures, enlarged prostate, tumor of the cervix, blood clots, acyclovir and uric acid. This group accounts for 10% of all cases presenting in outpatients with ARF (Thadhani *et al*, 1996), and typically the recovery rates are high as the problems are usually functional.

Figure 3.1: Stages of recovery following acute renal failure

Oliguric phase
(Drastic reduction in GRF < 400mls/24h with an increase in toxic solutes)
↓
Diuretic phase
(Filtration increases but tubular reabsorption is impaired, thus urine is dilute, stage may last from 10–14 days)
↓
Post diuretic phase
(Full recovery may last between 6 months to a year, during which time tubular properties return to normal)

For the patient with ARF, the progression to full recovery can be divided into three distinct stages as can be seen in *Figure 3.1*. However, optimal kidney recovery must involve structural healing and restoration of functional capacity. From the period of onset to the oliguric phase, urinary volume can fall as low as 5% and solute clearance drop to 10% of normal (Baer and Lancaster, 1992). During this stage oxygen consumption is also reduced to a quarter of health. With treatment and an improvement of renal blood flow, the diuretic phase follows resulting in an output of between 150–200%, but because the tubules are slowly regenerating the ability to reabsorb is still inadequate. This explains why urine volumes may be high but not concentrated, and why nitrogenous wastes in the blood may not be decreasing significantly. It is in the late and convalescence stages that serum biochemistry and haematology are restored, although full recovery may depend on pre-existing renal disease, age and other related factors. Toto (1992) claims that 5% of patients will develop chronic renal failure and will require long-term dialysis and a third will take a year to gain complete renal function.

Assessing the priorities for nursing care

In considering where the priorities of care lie for the patient with ARF, Norris (1989) suggests that this should be centred on preventing a deterioration in condition or where relevant forestalling development of this disease in those at risk. Baer and Lancaster (1992), agree that identifying those patients who are at danger of developing ARF is of concern, presumably because the severity of their illness places them under additional threat. This implies that an early assessment of the patient's clinical condition and initiating programmes of care which prevent or reduce the threat and consequence of ARF, is an imperative.

To manage patients in danger of developing ARF, accurate information about the individual's clinical health state is vital. Under close vigilance should be patients who require MV, who may have experienced episodes of sepsis or prolonged hypotension prior to ITU for whatever reason, who may have known risk factors and who may be of advancing age (Druml, 1996; Brivet *et al*, 1996). Similarly, in cardiac surgery patients, a reduced urine output during cardiopulmonary bypass, the need for intra-aortic balloon pump, and the age of the individual have all been noted to be independent risk factors of post-operative renal failure (Zanardo *et al*, 1994). Whereas pre-operative patient characteristics such as a reduced ejection fraction, circulation that is supported with an intra-aortic balloon pump, evidence of vascular disease and severe of heart failure have all been reported to be predictors of those who may develop ARF after heart surgery and have a poor prognostic outcome (Chertow *et al*, 1997).

In collecting the data for delivering the plan of care, the physical examination is paramount and should involve a review of fluid status. Depending on the severity, clinical assessment may reveal pulmonary, sacral and peripheral oedema, weight gain, the presence of a raised central venous pressure (CVP, normal 4–8cms of H_2O) and hypertension. If a pulmonary artery catheter is in place this is likely to show a pulmonary capillary wedge pressure of >18mmHg (normal PCWP 4–12mmHg) suggestive of congestion. A chest X-ray will also confirm the degree of pulmonary oedema.

Because of pulmonary oedema the unventilated patient may be short of breath, with a rapid and deep pattern of breathing (Kussmaul's sign) and so his/her mouth can be very dry. This pattern of respiration is a physiological response to the development of a metabolic acidosis. Thus in the acute phase arterial blood gas analysis will disclose a low pH and deranged bicarbonate reserves. Moreover, the level of pulmonary congestion may compromise the patient's gas exchange and adversely influence arterial oxygenation. If breathing spontaneously, the patient may be anxious and confused due to poor oxygenation and escalating uraemic levels.

With renal function damaged, the retention of certain electrolytes can also pose a threat to the patient's well being. Specifically, a rise in extracellular potassium >5.5 mmols/l (normal 3.5–5mmols/l) can be fatal, and demands urgent action because of the risks of ventricular dysrhythmias such as ventricular fibrillation and asytole are high. A review of the patient must also involve interpretation of the present cardiac rhythm, haematological screen, arterial blood gases, temperature trends as well as biochemical analysis of urine and blood, as together the information will provide a structure as to the patient's problems enabling the nurse to instigate actions that are either corrective, preventative or supportive (Catts, 1996; Norris, 1989).

To summarise, the general problems for the patient resulting from ATN, in addition to the underlying disease include:

- inability to regulate circulating volume resulting in accumulation of excess circulating fluid
- hypertension caused by disturbances of renin-angiotensin-aldosterone system
- incapacity to control acid-base imbalance leading to the retention of hydrogen ions and an inability to reabsorb bicarbonate ions
- cardiovascular instability due to altered electrolyte

balance (potassium and calcium)

- retention of nitrogenous waste products in the circulation
- depressed red cell formation (due to inability to release erythropoietin) and platelet dysfunction resulting from ARF.

Table 3.1: Priorities of care in the patient with acute renal failure requiring haemo(dia)filtration

Nursing priorities	Intervention/management
Optimising fluid balance	• haemodynamic monitoring (BP, CVP, PCWP) • accurate record of fluids • meet 24h prescribed fluid balance • consider effects of CRRT
Assessing for and correcting electrolyte imbalances	• ECG monitoring and interpretation • prescribed medications
Evaluation and correction of acid-base imbalance	• blood gas analysis • prescribed treatment
Preventing and controlling infection risks	• monitoring for signs of infection • preventative strategies
Maintenance of haemostasis	• assess puncture sites • analyse all losses
Restoring nutritional intake	• commence early • monitor
Maintenance of haemofiltration	• efficiency of system • patient safety • optimising treatment
Minimising psychological problems	• educating patients/families and creating a supportive environment

With newer forms of renal therapy such as continuous arterio/veno-venous haemofiltration (CAVH, CVVH), and haemodiafiltration (CAVHD or CVVHD), demands that actual and potential risks are rigourously assessed prior to treatment. Indeed, pivotal to the the plan of nursing care will be ensuring patient safety, maintaining the efficiency of extracorporeal system, and minimising potential complications.

Management of the patient's care

Patients with ARF typically present to an ITU as a result of a primary event but it is more likely that they develop this secondary to their underlying acute illness. While preventing complications and protecting the patient against life-threatening events, the precipitating illness must also be managed concurrently as this is also a priority (Morgan, 1996). Often, they may require a period of mechanical ventilation and sedation (Stevens and Rainford, 1992) and are dependent on skilled nursing interventions to ensure optimal recovery.

Optimising fluid balance

One of the patient's main problems will be an inability to regulate their own fluid status and they can present in an overloaded state, that may be as much as 2–5 litres (Lancaster, 1990; Norris, 1989). The initial treatment in these patients is through the use of diuretics (Conger, 1995). It would appear that many advocate the routine use of mannitol, an osmotic diuretic, as first choice as it is claimed to have direct benefits on damaged tubules, thereby preventing some forms of ARF (Myers and Moran, 1986; New and Barton, 1996). Alternatively, loop diuretics such as frusemide, that increase the movement of tubular fluid as well as inhibiting sodium reabsorption, are often prescribed although they may augment the nephrotoxicity of other drugs. Further, if used in combination with dopamine, it is argued that loop diuretics may assist in reversing ARF (Conger, 1995). However, with an improved understanding of the role of dopamine, its routine use in ARF either as a prophylatic agent or treatment, cannot be endorsed as the clinical evidence is limited and may produce adverse effects such as cardiac rhythm disturbances (New and Barton, 1996; Thadhani *et al*, 1996). Conger (1995) also concludes that due to a lack of controlled studies on the benefits of diuretics and dopamine as interventions for early or established ARF should preclude their broad use in clinical practice.

A few patients may be oliguric or anuric due to profound fluid loss or may be hypotensive due to sepsis, crash injuries, burns or hypovolaemic shock and may require aggressive fluid management with plasma expanders and inotropic support to stabilise and support cardiac output. In contrast, hypertension will be present in many patients due to disruption of the renin-angiotensin-aldosterone system as well as added volume loading. Commonly invasive monitoring of central venous pressure (CVP), PCWP and cardiac output are mandatory not only in estimating the circulating volume, but to inform on the effectiveness of treatment, and a means for anticipating patterns which may signpost deterioration or recovery (New and Barton, 1996).

If breathing spontaneously, the patient should be positioned sitting upright, supported by pillows to facilitate respiratory efforts, promote chest expansion and gas exchange. Likewise, comfort measures such as regular oral hygiene (due to breathlessness caused by acidosis) and humidified oxygen therapy will be important to the patient as well as preventing complications. Maintenance of skin integrity is also vital due to the lack of physical mobility, frailty of tissues, and catabolic and odematous changes that occur in these patients. Subsequently, an early risk assessment score should be performed and the appropriate strategies implemented, including turning schedules, providing nutritional support and the use of pressure relieving mattresses (Davies, 1995).

An hourly assesment of the CVP, PCWP and vital signs will provide the nurse with an index of fluid balance. However, the record of all the patient's intake (infusions, flushes and medications) and output (wound, rectal, urinary, and gastric) will enable nurses to estimate whether the prescribed 24-hour 'fluid' target will be achieved. When this data is combined with haemodynamic findings a realistic evaluation of circulating volume can be precisely determined. This is important, because hypovolaemia and hypervolaemia become major problems when CAVH/CVVH begins (Bosworth, 1992), as this involves balancing the hourly removal of plasma water from the patient's circulation and replacing this with an isotonic solution and nutritional supplements either with a similar or lesser volume. Moreover, the nurse should include the calculations of all other infusions, transfusions and losses to ensure balance is achieved. Nurses must therefore work closely with other key disciplines and plan the patient's 24-hour fluid balance so that this is restored without adverse consequences.

Assessing for and correcting electrolyte imbalances

Assessing for hyperkalaemia is generally through serum chemistry (>6.5mmol/litre), but specific changes in the PQRST complex can also be valuable. Although the most common hallmark of an ECG is a peaked T wave, there are other indexes of raised serum potassium that are evident on rhythm interpretation and these include:

- depressed ST segment
- loss of P wave
- wide QRS
- ventricular ectopics.

Correction of hyperkalaemia will be based on serum concentration. Immediate treatment includes an intravenous infusion of hypertonic dextrose and insulin which shifts the electrolyte back into the cells although the levels may be lowered rapidly by dialysis or CRRT. However, the management of hyperkalaemia may involve a combination of these approaches, though dialysis and continuous renal replacement therapies remain the favoured first line options for the critically ill patient (Burns *et al*, 1991; Davies, 1995; Thadhani *et al*, 1996). Yet even with CAVH, serum potassium levels require monitoring as these tend to fall significantly as a result of high volume exchanges (see below), thus additional supplements of 2–4mmol/litre may be required.

Other electrolytes which may have detrimental effects on the patient include hypocalcaemia and hyperphosphotaemia. With a low calcium concentration (normal 2.1–2.65 mmols/l) tetany, seizures, leg cramps, low cardiac output and cardiac dysrhythmias such as a prolonged QT interval or cardiac arrest may occur (Burns *et al*, 1991). As a result of ARF, the synthesis of vitamin D is compromised, this impedes the reaborption of calcium and accounts for the low serum levels. Restoration is achieved by a bolus dose of calcium gluconate or chloride and followed by a maintenance dose. Conversely, an elevated serum phosphate results due to failure of excretion, catabolism or tissue damage, and will also induce hypocalcaemia. However, serum phosphate is easily removed during haemofiltration and will require replacement. When organising the plan of care nurses must consider the relationship between electrolytes on a patient's symptoms and be aware of how these changes may be prevented or corrected.

Evaluation and correction of acid-base imbalance

Another concern in patients with ATN is that their kidneys are unable to reabsorb bicarbonate ions or to excrete acids, (ie. hydrogen ions) and this is manifested by a rapid respiratory rate, and cardiac irritability. The latter accumulate in the blood stream altering the pH and a metabolic acidosis ensues. To correct this instability, the body draws on plasma bicarbonate reserves in an effort to neutralise the degree of acidosis, and the respiratory rate also increases in order to expel acids and complement the buffering system. Assessment of a blood gas in a patient with ATN will illustrate either near normal PaO_2 arterial oxygenation (Tasota and Wesmiller, 1994) and the following:

pH	<7.3	(normal 7.35–7.45)
Bicarbonate	<20	(normal 24+/mmols/1)
$PaCO_2$	<4Kpa	(normal 4–5.5Kpa)
Base	<-4	(normal +/-2mmols)

However, the body's corrective processes will not last indefinitely and if the metabolic acidosis is not corrected, myocardial function may become depressed or irritable and hypotension will develop. This situation may equally worsen once treatment with haemofiltration commences, as this increases bicarbonate removal and reduces arterial pH, particularly in the presence of lactic acidosis (Forni and Hilton, 1997).

Treatment may involve an intravenous infusion of sodium bicarbonate but with attention to fluid and sodium loading as well as compatibility with other drugs (Burns *et al*, 1991; Forni and Hilton, 1997). It is also possible to dialyse against a bicarbonate solution, this ensures that bicarbonate ions move from the dialysis compartment into the circulation through diffusion and in this way correcting acidosis as well as assuring greater haemodynamic stability (Kirby and Davenport, 1996). Regular arterial blood gas analysis will provide evidence of whether the acidosis is improving.

Preventing and controlling infection risks

In over half of those with ARF their underlying problem may have been a septic event, but an associated impaired immune response is not untypical in these patients which in turn can jeopardise their well being further. The critical nature of their condition will often demand intense and invasive haemodynamic monitoring as such the risks of acquiring a hospital acquired infection are magnified. The nursing management of care should be directed at controlling and preventing the spread of secondary infection arising either from the illness and from intervention. Norris (1989) claims that chief sources for bacterial growth include the gastro-intestinal tract and the respiratory airways. Frequent position changes, chest physiotherapy, endo-tracheal suctioning, and the maintenance of patient hygiene are all preventative nursing manoeuvres. Rigorous asepsis, assessing for physical signs of infection, regular blood screening, wound swabbing and ensuring early adequate nutrition are also essential aspects of care. Strict aseptic techniques are also mandatory when manipulating the renal replacement circuit, when connecting patients to treatment and when cleaning access sites. Baer and Lancaster (1992) suggest that if the patient is anuric, the indwelling urinary catheter serves no purpose and should be removed. It is also appropriate that records of the length of time venous or arterial lines have been in place are kept and that where possible invasive options are curtailed.

Maintenance of haemostasis

Disruption of the haematological system is another problem for the patient which may be precipitated by a variety of factors including; an inability to produce erythropoietin, altered haematocrit due to due fluid overload, decreased life span of erythrocytes, loss of red blood cells due to filter clotting and the use of anticoagulants (Norris, 1989;Toto, 1992). In addition, the effects of raised metabolic waste products can depress platelet activity and delay the clotting time. As a consequence patients may be at risk of bleeding from various sites, for example at the entry of invasive lines, from trauma associated with urinary catheterisation or removal, and from repeated endotracheal suctioning. Nurses should therefore check all access/infusion sites for evidence of blood loss which should always be secured luer-lock connections. It is also important to evaluate for traces of occult loss this can be by testing gastric aspirate, urine and faeces.

Management for the anaemic patient may involve an infusion of packed cells, as the volume load is greatly reduced. In contrast, to prevent gastric bleeding due to stress ulceration or altered clotting time, prophylatic cytoprotective agents such as sucraflate or H_2 agonists may be administered. Equally, to minimise further disruption to the clotting mechanisms prior to commencing ultrafiltrative or dialytic therapies, it may be prudent to review the serum platelets as in many instances these may be reduced due to the presence of uraemic factors. Hence a loading and/or maintenance dose of anticoagulants prescribed to maintain the integrity of the circuit may not be required or only at reduced levels (Kirby and Davenport, 1996). However, if an infusion of heparin is prescribed this should be regularly checked and adjusted according to local guidelines.

Restoring nutritional intake

Many critically ill patients who develop ARF will become hypercatabolic and have need of at least 30kcal/kg/day, with most of this supplied by carbohydrates (Monson and Mehta, 1994; Morgan, 1996). Although glucose intake is also supplied through the metabolism of lactate found in substitution solutions, this is not generally realised (Barton and Hilton, 1993). In addition, amino acid administration should amount to 1g/kg/day to maintain or realise a positive nitrogen balance. Without early replacement the clinical picture may worsen and exacerbate metabolic problems, the risk of infections, muscle wastage, tissue healing and delay recovery. When the patient commences CAVH/CVVH or CAVHD, restriction of fluids and protein are less of a priority as serum biochemistry and circulating volume can be adjusted by the continuous removal of urea, creatinine, fluid and other waste products of metabolism. As such, the nutritional regime can include carbohydrates and proteins in large amounts, as well as daily minerals and trace elements so that the dietetic prescription meets the overall needs of the patient (Garrett, 1995). Weiss *et al* (1989), suggest that renal replacement therapies are advantageous in that they provide the means for ensuring a satisfactory hyperalimentation, preventing a discrepancy between catabolic demands and an ability to deliver balanced diet. However, where possible, the enteral route should be employed as it promotes gastric motility, reduces the risks of bacterial colonisation and minimises the incidence of complications associated with total parenteral nutrition.

There has been some debate recently about the value of early nutrition in this group of patients (Garrett, 1995; Sponsel and Conger, 1995). However, a recent analysis has concluded that immediate recognition of a patient's nutritional demands, adjustment of dietetic goals according to clinical condition and to forms of renal replacement therapy, can lead to a significant improvement in terms of recovery and in mortality rates (Monson and Mehta, 1994).

Maintenance of haemofiltration circuit

In the last decade, the development, simplicity and clinical application of continuous renal replacement therapies has progressed very rapidly, allowing ARF to be actively managed by intensivists and critical care nurses (Stevens and Rainford, 1992). The unique advantages of these forms of treatment have been identified and include:

- a gentle means of lowering raised urea and electrolytes without compromising cardiovascular function
- greater control over fluid balance, the gentle and continuous removal of large volumes of fluid, creating the space necessary for the administration of drug infusions, tranfusions and nutritional needs without detrimental effects on the systemic circulation. Further, for patients with a compromised haemo-

dynamic status, the large fluids shifts over a short period typical of haemodialysis would not be tolerated

• a flexible means of correcting acid-base imbalance, either by administering a buffer in the replacement fluid as in haemofiltration or counter-current to blood flow as in haemodiafiltration, or directly into a central line

• eliminating the problems of cerebral oedema or disequilibrium syndrome, (caused by the rapid removal of intracellular waste products) which has been associated with haemodialysis (Bihari and Beale, 1991)

• the avoidance of the need to transfer criticaly ill patients to regional centres, because no specialist medical or nursing expertise is required, they can be managed by intensivists (Walton *et al*, 1993).

Arteriovenous techniques, namely CAVH and CAVHD, rely chiefly on a patients' own arterial blood pressure to push blood flow around the extra-corporeal circuit in order to eliminate excess fluid and waste products. However, because the movement of blood relies solely on the patient's blood pressure, the removal of impurities and fluid is slow, as well as erratic. A drop in blood flow places the filter at greater risk of clotting and the loss of extra-corporeal circuit. In contrast with veno-venous methods, CVVH and CVVHD, a double lumen catheter provides the access instead and is placed in either the subclavian or femoral veins. Blood flow is continuously driven across the filter by means of a roller pump, this provides greater control over fluid and electrolyte losses. Additionally, the rapid circulating rates (100–250mls/min) increase filter lifespan because the risk of extra-corporeal circuit clotting is reduced (Barton *et al*, 1997; Canaud *et al*, 1988). Veno-venous techniques are also more suitable when arterial access is unsuitable or hazardous for the patient (Walton *et al*, 1993). Currently, in the UK, CVVH/D have become the most popular treatment modalities in ITUs (Stevens and Rainford, 1992).

Since the introduction of haemofiltration/diafiltration for the management of ARF and fluid overload states, the progression of these modalities has been employed for patients with hyperkalaemia, uncontrolled acidaemia (Barton *et al*, 1997), ARF complicated by septacaemia (Bellomo *et al*, 1993b), congestive heart failure unresponsive to conventional methods and for acute self poisonings. However, the literature is unclear as whether CVVH is suitable for all patients, or whether some patients are better managed with CVVHD.

Haemofiltration

Haemofiltration (*Figure 3.2*), is primarily concerned with the removal of fluid and secondly with solutes. It achieves this through two transport mechanisms, namely *ultrafiltration* and *convection*. The movement of plasma water from the circulation across a semi-permeable membrane is defined as ultrafiltration (UF), it is a passive process which relies on a positive pressure gradient created by the rate of blood flow. This pressure gradient may be further manipulated by lowering the drainage bag thus increasing the negative difference, or UF rate may be raised by placing pumps on the effluent tubing (Peachey *et al*, 1988). Waste products of middle molecular weight dissolved in the ultrafiltrate are dragged across the porous filter membranes, this is a process known as 'solvent drag' or convection. However, proteins and red blood cells remain in the circulation because of their larger molecular size (Barton and Hilton, 1993). It follows that when a sizeable volume of blood is filtered (1–2 litres/hour, 24–48 litres in 24 hours) there will be a corresponding rise in solute clearance through convective transfer and, Miller *et al*, (1990) suggest that at these rates urea clearance is around 9.5mls/min. To avoid a fluid deficit from the patient's circulation or triggering cardiac instability, a similar or slightly lesser amount is replaced (before or after the filter, *Figure 3.2*), depending on whether the patient is severely overloaded or whether 'space' is required to meet the nutritional needs.

This is unlike SCUF, slow continuous ultrafiltration, where the aim to reduce the circulating volume without substituting the losses. This process may involve removing 50–100mls/hour (1.2–2.4 litres over 24h) and patients may not be restricted in their oral intake.

Of recent interest has been the role of CVVH in the management of patients with septicaemic induced multi-organ failure (MOF) and effects on mortality rates. It is accepted that the presence of endotoxaemia triggers the release of

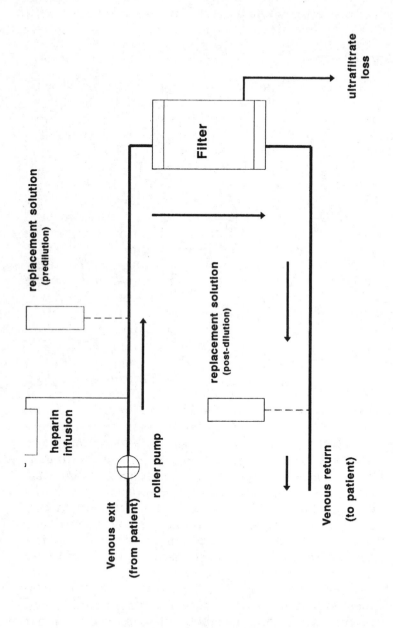

Figure 3.2: veno-venous haemofiltration

inflammatory cytokines (including tumor necrosing factor, interlukin, IL-1 and IL-6) which follow monocyte and neutrophyl activation. The consequences include endothelial cell damage, the release of other mediators that combine to precipitate a reduction in systemic vascular resistance and depress myocardial functioning. The continued rise of pro-inflammatory cytokines and vasoactive induced mediators will provoke profound hypotension, which will be typically managed by volume resuscitation, and the administration of adrenergic agents such as adrenaline, dopamine, noradrenaline and dobutamine (Kulkarni and Webster, 1996). However, it is now speculated that the early intervention of CVVH with high volume exchanges (48L/24 hours), may profit patients because the size of the haemofilter pores permits the clearance and extraction of cytokines from the blood stream. Substances with molecular weights of 20–30,000 daltons can be eliminated through the filter membrane and cytokines seem to fall within this range. This removal appears to translate to improved haemodynamic stability and survival rates in the more critically ill (Barzilay *et al*, 1989; Bellomo *et al*, 1993b; Storck *et al*, 1991). It is also suggested that the improvement may be due to the absorption of pro-inflammatory agents into the filter membranes (Journois *et al*, 1996; Kirby and Davenport, 1996). To date, the research in this area is limited although recent findings appear promising (Journois *et al*, 1996; van Bommel *et al*, 1995).

Haemodiafiltration

This is a process where *diffusive* transport mechanisms are central. Similar equipment as in haemofiltration is used, although running counter-current to the flow of blood is an isotonic solution that is pumped at 1–2L/hour to ensure that fresh dialysate is flowing continuously in the opposite direction (*Figure 3.3*). The physiological principle is that solutes found in high concentrations, urea creatinine and potassium, will diffuse from out of the circulation to an area of low concentration, namely the dialysate solution. This process impedes the passage of large and middle size molecules. Since this movement of electrolytes occurs down a concentration gradient, the need for a regular pumped supply of dialysate is vital. Moreover, this serves to augment the rapid transfer of smaller molecules so higher urea and

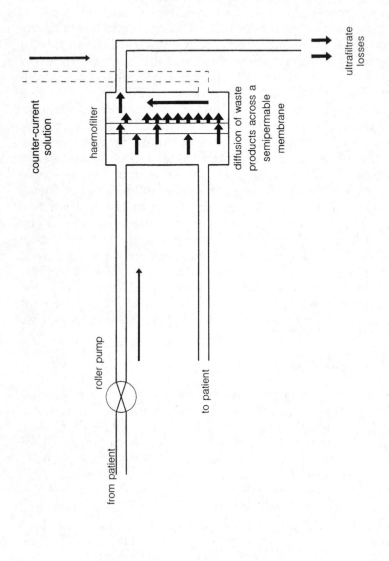

Figure 3.3: Veno-venous haemodiafiltration

creatinine clearances are achieved. The strategy behind using diafiltration is to control escalating rates solutes particularly for patients who are deemed to be highly catabolic (Bihari and Beale, 1991; Walton *et al*, 1993). While diffusion is the key transport mechanism in this system, convection also plays a role in the removal of toxic solutes.

Contemporary views as to the choice of modality seem to vary, Weiss *et al* (1989) and Van Geelen *et al* (1988) advocate that if serum urea exceeds 35mmol/l then CVVHD should be implemented as it has been demonstrated that higher urea clearances are achieved when compared with haemofiltration (Kox and Davies, 1992). A view that is supported by Miller *et al*, (1990) who note that with a flow rate 1 litre/h, urea levels can be maintained below 25mmols/l. This unlike CVVH which is more suited to treating patients with fluid overload, with a urea <25mmols/l (Weiss *et al,* 1989). Walton *et al,* (1993) have implied as much by placing overloaded states at one end of a continuum and highly catabolic at the opposite end (*Figure 3.4*). However, not all clinicians are in agreement. Forni and Hilton (1997) describe that they have succesfully managed 6000 ARF patients with CVVH and achieved a satisfactory metabolic control.

Figure 3.4: Continuum of continuous renal replacement therapies

Fluid overloaded states		Catabolic states	
SCUF	CVVH	CVVHD	AHF

The progression in the choice of modality should be based on an assessment of fluid state and solute toxicity. Therefore, in the mildly overloaded patient SCUF would be appropriate, for the individual with moderate acute renal syndrome CVVH would be suitable. In those with escalating and uncontrolled electrolytes it may be necessary to proceed with CVVHD, moreover with advancing automated systems (automated haemofiltration, AHF) it will be possible to alternate modalities according to the patient's clinical state.

From a nursing perspective there are a number of issues to be addressed when planning the delivery of care that will ensure optimal treatment, patient safety and prevent complications.

- To prevent fluid imbalance it is important to estimate the prescribed hourly balance and adjust fluids on the basis of a 24-hour regime, monitoring for potential fluid shifts, resulting in either hypovolaemia and hypervolaemia

- The use of CVP and pulmonary artery catheter readings, as well as blood pressure will also guide and support decisions. The frequent evaluation of haemodynamic parameters is essential, replacement fluids must be regulated accordingly to prevent derangements of circulating volume

- Prior to the administration of replacement fluids these should be warmed and the patients' temperature measured hourly. Other practical suggestions include insulating the lines with aluminium foil (Barton *et al*, 1997; Fox *et al*, 1996)

- Heparin infusion should be adjusted to achieve therapeutic range, normally 1½–2 the normal value, a progress record of bedside sampling will inform decision-making. Clotting parameters should be checked regularly and a full haematological screen obtained daily. Precautions need to be taken when changing the patient's position to prevent dislodgement of venous catheter and the access route must be checked for evidence of haematoma or trauma

- The maintenance of the extra-corporeal circuit integrity is a key responsibility, all connection sites should be checked at least once per shift. Additionally, the circuit must be examined for kinking, obstruction, and the filter ends inspected for evidence of discolouration of blood which is suggestive of clot formation. Other relevant observations include hourly measurement of ultrafiltrate, a decrease in this is also suggestive of clotting

- Maintenance of asepsis is also imperative at all stages, whether in priming the circuit during treatment and disposal of filter and lines. The access site must also be assessed for signs of infection, clear dressings allow inspection. Temperature should be recorded and signs of pyrexia should be reported

- Biochemistry assessment is also crucial, particularly

potassium, sodium, calcium, magnesium, bicarbonate and phosphate as these will require replacement since they are removed from the plasma (Forni and Hilton, 1997). Evaluation of blood gases will, in contrast, determine whether the metabolic acidosis is improving

- Skin integrity should be regularly scrutinised as patients' mobility will be limited due to the treatment. Additionally, distal pulses, colouration and temperature should be checked if femoral access is in use

- Drugs which typically accumulate in the circulation as a result of ARF are removed during haemofiltration. Medication dosage and administration times may have to be adjusted to ensure optimal levels and prevent sub-therapeutic treatment (Davies *et al*, 1995; Foster *et al*, 1996; Forni and Hilton, 1997)

- Written protocols must be developed in collaboration with medical staff defining areas of nursing responsibility (Hagland, 1994; Lievaart and Voerman, 1991; Pinson, 1992; Price, 1989).

Maintaining filter performance and optimising treatment are also major challenges, but this can be augmented through pre-dilution techniques. The administration of low dose heparin in the arterial limb of the circuit prevents the extra-corporeal circuit from clotting although, in practice, reaching optimal range can be problematic (Bihari and Beale, 1991) partly because the removal of filtrate will lead to concentration of red blood cells and plasma proteins resulting in raised blood viscocity and oncotic pressure at the distal end of the filter. Replacing fluid on the arterial side prior to the filter has numerous advantages. For example, it is suggested that the delivery of substitution fluid when mixed with blood decreases the haematocrit and resistance of blood flow. As a result of reduced viscosity, together with the increased blood flows rates, filter clotting will be less likely and it is also possible to lower the amount of anticoagulants prescribed (Kaplan, 1985; Barton *et al*, 1997). Moreover, the presence of increased plasma water creates a gradient with the uraemic blood, and for this reason a diffusive process is set up that allows the passage of urea out of the red cells into the plasma and, as a result, urea clearance rates are doubled to around 17mls/min (Golper *et al*, 1988; Kaplan, 1985). However, the main disadvantage with this approach, is that many essential electrolytes are lost in the ultrafiltrate and these have to be replaced by means of intravenous infusions. This adds to the costs and increases the number of syringe drivers and equipment at the bedside. Forni and Hilton (1997) advise, that to overcome the problem of haemoconcentration and high colloid pressures, maintaining the filtration rate to 30% of blood flow rate should minimise this. Clearly, the responsibilities of the nurse are diverse and wide, and a theoretical understanding is vital to guarantee that the patient's care and needs, are intelligently managed (Bosworth, 1992).

Minimising psychological problems

For many critically ill individuals and their families the added concern over the patient's renal function as well as underlying condition, can stretch coping strategies and emotional reserve. This can be compounded by the complexity of the technology at the bedside and the prospect of delayed recovery or even the need for long-term haemodialysis. Stark (1994) suggests that family and patients' emotions may fluctuate between despair and hope, in some cases their worries may be exaggerated or based on misconceptions and misunderstandings particularly during the early stages of the diagnosis. Nurses must therefore ensure that they provide continued and appropriate information tailored to meet the patient and families' needs. Explanations about the purpose of the treatment and expected changes resulting from the intervention should also be included. Photographic displays or illustrations of CVVH or CCVHD prior to treatment and details about the various safety alarms can help patients/ families to understand and conceptualise the nature of the array of extra technology and may assist in minimising additional anxiety. Patients and significant others should be encouraged to express their feelings and anxieties, but this can only be secured if the unit atmosphere is supportive and creates a sense of openness, honesty and trust. For many patients, the length of stay on ITU may be long and so nurses should encourage family participation in appropriate aspects of care. Engaging in providing such care for loved ones, can be viewed as a source of comfort and doing something positive. Frequent visits, personal belongings by the bedside and encouraging communication from family members, whether verbal or non-verbal all serve to promote the uniqueness of the individual.

References

Baer CL, Lancaster L (1993) Acute renal failure. *Crit Care Nurs Q* **14**(4): 1–21

Barton IK, Hilton PJ (1993) Veno-venous haemofiltration in the intensive care unit. *Clin Intensive Care* **4**(1): 16–22

Barton IK, Barton J, Chesser A (1997) Haemofiltration: How to do it. *Br J Hosp Med* **57**(5): 188–193

Barzilay E, Kessler D, Berlot G *et al* (1989) Use of extracorporeal supportive techniques as additional treatments for septic-induced multiple organ failure patients. *Crit Care Med* **17**(7): 634–637

Bellomo R, Noyce N (1993a) Does continuous haemofiltration improve survival in acute renal failure? *Semin Dialysis* **6**(1):16–19

Bellomo R, Tipping P, Boyce N (1993b) Continuous veno-venous haemofiltration with dialysis removes cytokines from the circulation of septic patients. *Crit Care Med* **21**(4): 522–526

Bihari D, Beale R (1991) Renal support in the Intensive Care Unit. *Curr Opin Anaes* **4**: 272–278

Bosworth C (1992) SCUF/CAVH/CAVHD: Critical differences. *Crit Care Nurs Q* **14**(4): 45–55

Brivet F, Kleinknecht D, Loirat P *et al* (1996) Acute renal failure in intensive care units — Causes, outcome, and prognostic factors of hospital mortality: A prospective multi-centre study. *Crit Care Med* **24**(2): 192–198

Burns K, Ismail N, Helderman J *et al* (1991) Urgent problems in the renal patient. In: Levine D (ed) *Care of the renal patient* (2nd edn). WB Saunders, Philadelphia

Canaud B, Garred L, Christol JP *et al* (1988) Pump assisted continuous veno-venous haemofiltration for treating acute uraemia. *Kidney Int* **33**(Suppl 24): s154–s156

Catts L (1996) Assessment and diagnostic procedures. In: Urden L, Lough ME, Stacy K (eds) *Priorities in critical care nursing* (2nd edition). Mosby, St. Louis

Chertow GM, Lazarus JM, Christianssen C *et al* (1997) Preoperative renal risk stratification. *Circulation* **95**: 878–884

Conger J (1995) Interventions in clinical acute renal failure: What are the data. *Am J Kidney Dis* **26**(4): 565–576

Davies A (1995) Acute renal failure due to drug-induced rhabdomyolosis. *Br J Nurs* **4**(13): 771–774

Davies JG, Kingswood J, Sharpstone P *et al* (1995) Drug removal in continuous haemofiltration and haemodialysis. *Br J Hosp Med* **54**(10): 524–528

Druml W (1996) Prognosis of acute renal failure, 1975–1995. *Nephron* **73**: 8–15

Forni LG, Hilton P (1997) Continuous haemofiltration in the treatment of acute renal failure. *New Eng J Med* **336**(18): 1303–1309

Foster P, Gordon F, Holloway S (1996) Drug adjustment during continuous renal replacement therapy. *Br J Intensive Care* **6**: 120–124

Fox H, Martin PY, Stoermann C (1996) Heat losses associated with continuous veno-venous haemofiltration in intensive care patients. *Clin Intensive Care* **6**: 266–268

Garret B (1995) The nutritional management of acute renal failure. *J Clin Nurs* **4**: 377–382

Golper T, Ronco C, Kaplan A (1988) Continuous arteriovenous haemofiltration: improvements, modifications and future directions. *Semin Dialysis* **1**(1): 50–54

Hagland M (1994) Making sense of continuous renal replacement therapy. *Nurs Times* **90**(40): 37–39

Hulman P, Wolfson M (1993) The patient with acute renal failure. *Hosp Med* **29**(7): 82–89, 93–95

Journois D, Israel-Biet D, Pouard P *et al* (1996) High-volume, zero balanced haemofiltration to reduced delayed inflamatory response to cardiopulmonary bypass in children. *Anaes* **85**(5): 965–975

Kaplan AA (1985) Pre-dilution versus post-dilution for CAVH. *Trans-American Society of Artificial Internal Organs* **31**: 28–32

Kirby S, Davenport A (1996) Haemofiltration/dialysis treatment in patients with acute renal failure. *Care Crit Ill* **12**(2): 54–58

Kulkarni V, Webster N (1996) Management of sepsis. *Care Crit Ill* **12**(4): 122–127

Kox W, Davies SP (1992) Continuous haemodialysis in the critically ill. *Care Crit Ill* **8**(1): 8–11

Lancaster LE (1990) Renal response to shock. *Crit Care Nurs Clinics North America* **2**(2): 221–233

Leaker B (1988) Acute renal failure. *Care Crit Ill* **4**(3): 6–9

Liaño F, Garcia-Martin F, Gallego A *et al* (1989) Easy and early prognosis in acute tubular necrosis: A Forward analysis of 228 cases. *Nephron* **51**: 307–313

Lievaart A, Voerman HJ, (1991) Nursing management of continuous arteriovenous haemodialysis. *Heart Lung* **20**(2): 152–160

Meyers B, Moran SM (1986) Haemodynamically mediated acute renal failure. *New Eng J Med* **314**(2): 97–105

Miller R, Kingswood C, Bullen C *et al* (1990) Renal replacement therapy in the ICU: The role of continuous arteriovenous haemofiltration. *Br J Hosp Med* **43**: 354–362

Monson P, Mehta R (1994) Nutrition in acute renal failure: A reappraisal for the 1990s. *J Renal Nutrition* **4**(2): 58–77

Morgan A (1996) The management of acute renal failure. *Br J*

Hosp Med **55**(4): 167–170
New DI, Barton IK (1996) Prevention of acute renal failure. *Br J
Hosp Med* **55**(4): 162–166
Norris MK (1989) Acute tubular necrosis: Preventing
complications. *Dimensions Crit Care Nurs* **8**(1): 16–26
Peachey T, Ware R, Eason J *et al* (1988) Pump control of
continuous arteriovenous haemofiltration. *Lancet*: ii, 878
Pinson J (1992) Preventing complications in the CAVH patient.
Dimensions Crit Care Nurs **11**(5): 242–248
Price C (1989) Continuous arteriovenous ultrafiltration: A
monitoring guide for ICU nurses. *Crit Care Nurse* **9**(1):
12–19
Price C (1994) Acute renal failure: A sequelae of sepsis. *Crit
Care Nurs Clinics North America* **6**(2): 359–372
Sponsel H, Conger JD (1995) Is parenteral nutrition therapy of
value in acute renal failure patients? *Am J Kidney Dis* **25**(1):
96–102
Stark J (1994) Acute renal failure in trauma: Current
perspectives. *Crit Care Nurs Q* **16**(4): 49–60
Stevens PE, Rainford DJ (1992) Continuous renal replacement
therapy: Impact on the management of acute renal failure.
Br J Intensive Care **2**(8): 361–369
Storck M, Hartl W, Zimmerer E *et al* (1991) Comparison of
pump-driven and spontaneous haemofiltratin on
post-operative acute renal failure. *Lancet* **337**: 452–455
Tasota F, Wesmiller S (1994) Assessing ABGs: maintaining the
delicate balance. *Am J Nurs*: 34–44
Thadhani R, Pascual M, Bonventre JV (1996) Acute renal
failure. *New Eng J Med* **334**(22): 1448–1459
Toto KH (1992) Acute renal failure: A question of Location. *Am
J Nurs* **92**: 44–53
Van Bommel E, Bouvy N, So K *et al* (1995) Acute dialytic
support for the critically ill: Intermittent haemodialysis
versus continuous arteriovenous haemodiafiltration. *Am J
Nephrol* **15**: 192–200
Van Geelen JA, Vincent HH, Schalekamp MA (1988) Continuous
arteriovenous haemofiltration and haemodiafiltration in
acute renal failure. *Nephrol Dial Transplant* **2**: 181–186
Walton P, Hamilton M, Hattersley J *et al* (1993) Continuous
arteriovenous haemofiltration an inappropriate therapy.
EDTNA J XIX(4): 31–33
Weiss L, Danielson BG, Wirkström B *et al* (1989) Continuous
arteriovenous haemofiltration in the treatment of 100
critically ill patients with renal failure: report on clinical
outcome and nutritional aspects. *Clin Nephrol* **31**(4):
184–189
Woodrow G, Turney JH (1992) Cause of death in acute renal
failure. *Nephrol Dialysis Transplantation* **7**: 230–234
Zanardo G, Michielon P, Paccagnella A *et al* (1994) Acute renal
failure in the patient undergoing cardiac operation. *J
Thorac Cardiovasc Surg* **107**(6):1489–1495

4

Managing the nursing priorities in the patient with a cerebral insult

Introduction

The objectives of this chapter are;

- to discuss the pathophysiological changes that occur following severe head injury and a cerebrovascular incident
- to discuss effective strategies of assessing and managing the priorities of care following severe cerebral insult
- to discuss the complications that may arise as a result of a severe cerebral insult.

Approximately half a million people with head injuries are seen each year by the health care system in the United Kingdom. Of these about 10% are admitted to intensive care for management (Pickard, 1993, cited by Jeevaratnam, 1996). Not all patients with severe neurological dysfunction who are admitted to intensive care have severe head injuries. Cerebral oedema can also occur during prolonged cardiac arrest or as a result of electrolyte and fluid imbalance caused by drug overdose, near drowning or severe liver disease. Other major causes of death in the western world arise from subarachnoid haemorrhage and stroke. As this group, and those patients who have sustained severe head injuries, form the largest proportion of patients who are suffering from a neurological dysfunction who are admitted to general and neurological intensive care units, this chapter will specifically focus on their nursing management.

Causative factors and patient problems

Volume

Brain tissue, cerebral blood volume and cerebro spinal fluid (CSF) form the three components located within the rigid structure of the skull, all of which contribute to an intracranial pressure. According to the Kellie-Monro hypothesis changes in volume to any of these components will cause spatial compensation of the others. Therefore, if cerebral oedema develops and brain tissue volume increases, the ventricles may partially collapse, CSF production may reduce, absorption can increase and venous blood can be diverted out of the cranium. The compliance of the system, enables small increases in volume without causing large rises in intracranial pressure. However, these compensatory mechanisms are limited, once a critical increase in brain volume occurs, compensatory redistribution of blood and CSF is severely limited. At this point the rising intracranial pressure will shift brain tissue, displace the ventricles and reduce circulating flow to compressed tissue. This will lead to ischaemic changes and death of neural tissue.

Intracranial pressure is frequently monitored in patients within the intensive care setting. Its assessment contributes to determining effective management strategies and warning of neurological deterioration. In health ICP values exist between 0–15 mm Hg changes in pressure occur in response to factors such as sneezing, rapid eye movement sleep, straining and position.

Cerebral blood flow

Cerebral blood flow is controlled by the process known as autoregulation. A constant flow at 50 mL/100 g per minute is maintained by the tight control exerted over the cerebrovasculature. The extent of vasoconstriction and dilation will match the supply and demand needs of metabolism (Pollack-Latham, 1987). Local factors that regulate cerebrovascular resistance are listed in *Table 4.1*.

Mean systemic arterial blood pressure (MAP) is a systemic influencing factor. Rises in MAP will increase intraluminal pressures of the cerebral arteries. In response, the cerebral arteries constrict to prevent blood being delivered to brain tissue at high pressure.

Table 4.1: Chemical factors affecting cerebrovasculature and cerebral blood flow

Arterial carbon dioxide
Cerebral metabolic rate of oxygen
Volume of oxygen in arterial blood
pH
Neurotransmitters, eg. acetylcholine, prostaglandins, serotonin
Catecholamines
(Prociuk, 1995)

A severe cerebral insult can interfere with autoregulation, which results in a loss of control over the cerebral vasculature, with blood flow and cerebral perfusion pressure (CPP) passively following systemic blood pressure. As a result, increases in blood pressure will be accompanied by increases in cerebral blood flow and an increase in ICP. Rises in ICP and CPP may breakdown the blood brain barrier causing the development of cerebral oedema. Conversely, in the presence of altered autoregulation, if CPP falls then cerebral blood flow will decline and the oxygen supply will be inadequate resulting in ischaemia (Prociuk, 1995).

Cerebrovascular spasm is a major complication of subarachnoid haemorrhage (SAH) and occurs between 2–10 days following the primary bleed (Rusy, 1996) The incidence of spasm appears to increase in the presence of thick diffuse subarachnoid blood which is thought to release prostaglandins, catecholamines, serotonin and oxyhaemoglobin, when the clot degenerates (Rusy 1996). These vasoactive substances may interfere with calcium transport resulting in high intracellular levels of calcium which cause vessel wall spasm.

Cerebral perfusion pressure

Cerebral perfusion pressure (CPP) is the cerebral blood flow pressure. In health brain cell tissue it is perfused at a CPP between 75–100 mmHg. However, adequate perfusion exists at 60 mmHg but at less than 50 mmHg results in cerebral ischaemia (Pollack-Latham, 1987; Prociuk, 1995).

Classification of head injury

The acceleration and deceleration forces that occur during trauma can cause disruption of brain tissue.The stretching and shearing of white fibres causes diffuse axonal injury, the brain may be contused and haemorrhage results from the traumatic rupture of blood vessels. *Table 4.2* lists the types of injury seen and illustrate the impact of cerebral functioning and implications for cerebral monitoring.

Table 4.2: Types of head and structural changes

Type of injury	
Skull fracture	Can be linear, depressed or compound and may result in underlying brain injury. Base-of-skull fractures can lead to CSF leaking through the sinuses from the subarachnoid space out of nose or ear passages. Bacterial contamination risks are high.
Cerebral concussion	Forces to brain during trauma were minor, causing mild diffuse brain injury. Person may lose consciousness briefly and is amnesic of event.
Cerebral contusion	The brain is bruised from the shock waves that spread through it following impact. The brain tissue is not lacerated but there is a small haemorrhage which has diffused through the area of impact.
Axonal injury	Disruption of white fibres from the forces of the impact. Causes microscopic diffuse haemorrhages and axonal damage. Autonomic dysfunction often follows causing, hypertension, fever and sweating.

Subdural haematoma	The tearing of surface veins and disruption to venous sinuses results in a collection of blood below the dura and above the arachnoid layer. Commonly occur in temporal lobe. Subdural collections can also occur more slowly in patients who have clotting disturbances.
Extradural haematoma	Tearing of the middle or frontal meningeal artery in the temporal-parietal area can lead to extradural haematoma formation. Blood accumulates between the skull and the outer layer of the meninges. This group sometimes called 'talk and die' as they classically lose consciousness for a few seconds then appear lucid for minutes to hours. Period then follows of rapid neurological deterioration.
Intracerebral haematoma	Forces that cause an intracerebral collection have usually been severe. Describes a collection of blood located within brain tissue, but is commonly seen with a subdural haematoma.
Contrecoup	Damage occurs to the area of brain that meets with primary impact, but damage also occurs on opposite side as brain hits skull during the rebound.

Cerebral trauma that results in cerebral oedema and or a collection of blood will increase intracranial pressure and reduce cerebral perfusion resulting in hypoxia of nerve cell tissue. Clinical signs of a rising intracranial pressure are:

- headache
- restlessness, disorientation, lethargy
- motor dysfunction.

If the raised ICP is untreated, or if measures are ineffective, brain herniation may occur causing compression on the cranial nerves and brain stem. The following signs may then be seen:

- changes in pupillary reactivity and size
- deteriorating conscious level

- Cushing's response — due to brain stem compression
- decreased respiratory rate
- decreased heart rate
- increased systolic blood pressure
- increased pulse pressure (Hickey, 1992).

Cerebrovascular bleed/clots

Subarachnoid haemorrhage is usually caused by the rupture of an intracranial aneurysm. Ruptured arteriovenous malformation, and hypertensive cerebral haemorrhage can also cause bleeding into the subarachnoid space. Blood may also track into the subdural space, the ventricles and the basal cisterns (Rusy, 1996).

Blood within the subarachnoid space will cause meningeal irritation and the development of a number of signs and symptoms. The signs and symptoms have been graded into a classification scale by Hunt and Hess (1968), *Table 4.3* is used to evaluate the severity of the bleed and changes in the patients condition.

Table 4.3: Classification of subarachnoid haemorrhage

Grade	Symptoms
I	Mild headache
II	Mild to moderate headache, neck rigidity, cranial nerve palsy
III	Drowsiness, confusion or mild focal deficit
IV	Moderate to severe hemiparesis, decorticate, decerebrate posturing, depressed level of consciousness
V	Coma, decerebrate posturing, moribund
(Adapted from Hunt and Hess, 1968, cited by Rusy, 1996)	

One of the major complications of a subarachnoid bleed is rebleeding. This is due either to increases in systemic blood pressure or initiated by the release of vasoactive chemicals from the dissolving clot. Rebleeding can occur between the third and eleventh day, but the peak incidence occurs on day seven (Rusy, 1996).

Acute complications of head injury and cerebral vascular bleed

There are many complications that may arise as a result of serious neurological dysfunction in the long term recovery period such as; communication difficulties, sensory and motor deficit or behavioural problems. Patients managed within the intensive care setting may also develop complications that arise from their management. For example, pulmonary stasis can lead to pneumonia, infection may develop because of the use of invasive lines or inadequate nutrition due to gastric stasis induced by the use of opiates and relaxants. However, the following acute complications can also occur:

1. Brain herniation leading to brain stem death

2. Neurogenic pulmonary oedema

3. Seizure activity

4. Hyperthermia.

Brain herniation, sometimes termed 'coning' occurs in response to a rapidly increasing intracranial mass. Tentorial or uncal herniation describes the situation where increased pressure caused by an expanding mass above the tentorium (a dural extension) pushes sections of the cortex through the hiatus in the tentorium into the posterior fossa. This causes displacement and compression of the brain stem, that may then be displaced through the foramen magnum. Brain herniation may be central or unilateral (Jennett and Teasdale, 1984). The result is death of brain tissue caused by the compression and blood supply to the brain stem may be reduced or cease. Vital functions, respiratory and cardioregulatory, controlled by the brain stem will be impaired.

Neurogenic pulmonary oedema can develop in response to the initiation of the Cushing response. A rise in intracranial pressure activates the sympathetic nervous system which increases systemic blood pressure by inducing vasoconstriction. More blood is shunted through to the lower pressure pulmonary vasculature, which increases hydrostatic pressure and fluid leaks from capillaries into alveoli. Pulmonary oedema will reduce oxygen and carbon dioxide transport, thereby increasing the risk of hypoxia and hypercarbia which will cause cerebral vasodilation and

increased cerebral blood flow leading to further rise in ICP
(Jennett and Teasdale, 1984).

Seizure activity in the acute stages following a cerebral
insult is relatively common. The electrical activity may be
focal in nature causing only one part of the body to convulse
or activity may be global causing a generalised convulsion.
Increased electrical activity may be initiated as a result of
hypoxia and brain damage. Further brain damage can occur
due to hypoxia if fitting is not controlled (Buzea, 1995).

Assessing the priorities for nursing care

Effective management of patients in the acute phase
requires continuous monitoring of a number of parameters.
Table 4.4 identifies specific parameters that require
consideration.

Table 4.4: Assessing the priorities for nursing care

Patient problems	Assessment method
Cerebral impairment	1. Glasgow coma scale/score 2. Pupils 3. ICP/CPP monitoring 4. Cerebral oximetry 5. Mixed jugular venous oxygen saturation monitoring 6. Transcranial doppler 7. EEG 8. CT scan, MRI, angiogram
Respiratory disturbances	Blood gas analysis Ventilation control methods Respiratory function
Cardiovascular instability	Arterial blood pressure, heart rate Central venous pressure Blood chemistry to establish electrolyte balance and fluid needs Nutritional assessment pH stability
Thermoregulation imbalance	Continuous temperature monitoring Evaluate impact on other body systems if active hypothermia is used

Assessment methods of cerebral function

Glasgow coma scale

This scale involves assessment of 3 parameters:

- motor response
- verbal response
- eye opening response.

Using a predetermined stimulus, eg. calling the person's name, touch or pain, the person's best response in each of these categories is observed and charted. A score can then be calculated — as each response on the scale is graded according to the degree of dysfunction. The frequency of the assessment usually diminishes as the patient improves, but can be performed at 15–30 minute intervals during the initial critical period.

The scale was designed in 1974 by Teasdale and Jennett and appears to have gained international acceptance in assessing acute neurological dysfunction.The scale also contributed to a recognised standardisation of the term coma. Coma is said to exist if a patient scores less than 8. Twenty years on since its design the tool has been incorporated into scoring systems that are used to predict outcome. The scale is also widely used by paramedics, medical and nursing staff to assess neurological dysfunction. This may be because of its perceived ease of use. The designers proposed that little experience or training was required to use the tool effectively (Teasdale, 1975). This appears to be supported by nursing research, which agrees that reliability in the use of the scale can be demonstrated (Fielding and Rowley, 1990; Juarez and Lyons, 1995). Agreement rates between staff in an intensive care setting were found to be 'moderate to high'. However, there has been the suggestion that what contributes to the tool's effective use is education and experience. These are factors that gain support from Ellis and Cavanagh (1992) who found that disagreement rates were higher between junior staff and experienced trained personnel. Nevertheless, difficulties exist in the use of the tool in the intensive care setting (Price, 1996). It is difficult to assess effectively the sedated, ventilated head injured patient who may also have serious limb and facial trauma (Ingersoll and Leyden, 1987).

Investigations into the tool's use in this group of patients appears to be limited and warrants further exploration (Robinson, 1992). Another problem in the use of the GCS is that by design it is used intermittently and so does not provide the intensive care nurse with a continuous account of the patient's neurological status. Interpretation of a deterioration in status may therefore go undetected for 30–60 minutes, precious time in the early stages of critical head injury. It is also flawed in that by the time clinical deterioration is apparent by a change in one of the parameters, secondary damage may already have occurred. It may then be too late to reverse the damage (McCormick *et al*, 1991).

Pupils

The pupils are controlled by the oculomotor nerve. Compression of this nerve by swollen or damaged tissue can result in a fixed dilated pupil. Pupil assessment is usually conducted at the same as the Glasgow coma scale assessment. The pupil is examined for:

- size (in millimetres)
- reactivity to light
- shape
- equality.

Normally, pupils will constrict when light is shone directly onto the eye. The size of the pupil (1–8mm) and its reactivity can then be charted.

Intracranial pressure monitoring

The patient who has sustained a serious cerebral insult may lose the ability to compensate for changes to one or more of the three cerebral components. In this event ICP will rise. A sustained elevated ICP will reduce cerebral perfusion pressure (CPP) and can cause herniation of the damaged tissue into another cerebral compartment. The pressure this exerts coupled with reduced oxygen delivery from the fall in CPP will cause further ischaemia and secondary damage. Aggressive monitoring and management of the ICP and CPP are essential components of caring for the patient who has received a serious cerebral insult (Pollack-Latham, 1987).

ICP and CPP monitoring can be achieved by using a

number of devices, although disposable fibreoptic monitors appear to be replacing the fluid filled systems that have an external transducer (Kapadia and Jha, 1995). Fibreoptic devices are calibrated at time of manufacture and are zeroed at time of insertion. Placement of the device can be in one of 4 areas:

- intraventricular — usually the lateral ventricle. This is considered to be the 'gold standard'. Intra-ventricular monitoring can also be coupled with a ventricular drain which facilitates the drainage of CSF
- an extradural sensor that is placed between the skull and the dura
- subdural/subarachnoid placement — sensor in either space
- intraparenchymal placement — sensor located in brain substance.

Usually the sensor will be placed on the uninjured side of the brain, although this may vary in some centres. Information obtained from either of the lateral ventricles is thought to be reliable as little differences in pressure have been found (Kapadia and Jha, 1995). Acknowledgement of the benefits of ICP and CPP monitoring is widespread. It enables recognition of intracranial hypertension, early aggressive treatment and improved outcome. Complications, though, such as infection and haemorrhage have been reported (Eddy *et al,* 1995). However, these appear to be associated with fluid filled systems, where breaks in the system may inadvertently allow the introduction of bacteria.

Cerebral perfusion pressure monitoring

Following severe head injury a number of complex mechanisms that involve dynamic changes to ICP, CPP and cerebral blood flow come into play. In the past it has been difficult to measure cerebral blood flow at the bedside. Due to its close interrelationship with cerebral perfusion pressure and mean arterial pressure, cerebral blood flow is indirectly measured by monitoring CPP. Cerebral perfusion pressure is simultaneously monitored with ICP and mean arterial pressure (MAP). However unlike ICP, the measurement of CPP is not a direct measure, it is a gross estimate of cerebral blood pressure. The accurate calculation of CPP requires the measurement of cerebral blood flow and cerebrovascular resistance. Within the intensive care unit, CPP is usually indirectly established using the calculation; CPP=MAP-ICP. CPP, blood flow and cerebrovascular resistance are closely linked together by the processes of autoregulation. In severe brain injury loss of autoregulation of the cerebrovasculature can occur. This means that cerebral blood flow passively follows cerebral perfusion pressure due to a fixed cerebrovascular resistance. These processes are difficult to determine when measuring CPP indirectly. Maintaining the CPP at 60 mmHg or above may not actually be sufficient in preventing cerebral ischaemia. Another major disadvantage of CPP monitoring is that it reflects global perfusion and so does not provide information about cerebral oxygenation or cerebrovascular haemo-dynamics in specific areas of the brain. Patients with severe brain injury may have varying degrees of altered autoregulation; therefore care needs to be taken in interpreting a relatively good perfusion pressure in the presence of a severe head injury.

Laser doppler flowmetry

Cortical perfusion pressure can be established using laser doppler flowmetry (LDF). This technique involves the insertion of a fibreoptic probe which is inserted through the skull to sit under the dura on the surface of the cortex. Laser light is delivered through the probe onto the cerebral microvasculature. The LDF probe measures red cell concentration and velocity which are components of the final measurement — microcirculatory red cell flux, or micro-circulatory flow. This measure of regional blood flow closely correlates with cerebral perfusion pressure enabling comparisons to be made when management or the patients state of autoregulation change (Kirkpatrick *et al*, 1994). Kirkpatrick *et al* found that autoregulation appears to fail at CPP values that were less than 58 mmHg. However, Kirkpatrick *et al* also found that there were problems in using LDF in the clinical area. A major problem arose due to difficulties in maintaining a constant probe position, any movement would cause the light to scatter which would alter the signal.

Transcranial doppler sonography

Transcranial doppler sonography (TCD) is widely used to determine the cerebral haemodynamics of patients undergoing cerebrovascular surgery and vascular spasm. Pulses of ultrasonic energy are directed, non invasively, through the thinnest sections of the cranium onto the moving red blood cells in the anterior and posterior circulation. The reflected signal is transduced to form a waveform that is used to determine blood flow velocities and the calculation of a pulsatility index which reflects cerebrovascular resistance (Lucke *et al*, 1995; Fearon and Rusy, 1994; Miller *et al*, 1994). The pulsatility index will usually remain constant when CPP is maintained at 70 mmHg, although will rise if CPP falls. A major advantage of this system is that it can provide an early warning of impending ischaemia due to vasospasm or low flow, and is relatively easy to use at the bedside. It has also been used in a number of studies to evaluate the effects head injury has on cerebral haemodynamics. Blood flow velocities do have to be interpreted with care as a number of variables impinge on their value. Age, sex and haematocrit all influence blood flow velocity. Anatomical factors such as vessel angle and size can also alter the value. Another problem in its use is that it appears to be subject to user error which may be amplified during serial measurements (Fearon and Rusy, 1994).

Jugular bulb monitoring of mixed venous oxygen saturation

The maintenance of cerebral function crucially depends on the adequate supply of oxygen to the brain. Therefore, cerebral oxygen supply and demand parameters together with cerebral responsiveness to carbon dioxide are of interest when monitoring cerebral haemodynamics. The insertion of a fibreoptic catheter into the jugular bulb via the internal jugular vein can facilitate the continuous measurement of mixed jugular venous oxygen saturation. This measurement can contribute to determining the global state of oxygenation in the brain (Miller *et al*, 1994; Fortune *et al*, 1994; Sheinberg *et al*, 1992; Cruz *et al*, 1991; Williams *et al*, 1994a).

Jugular venous oxygen saturation monitoring can determine the effectiveness of treatment for intracranial hypertension. Cerebral hypoxia as indicated by a jugular venous saturation ($SjvO_2$) of less than 50% may occur during the use of hyperventilation which causes cerebral vaso-constriction. Ventilation can therefore be adjusted to allow the $PaCO_2$ to rise and reduce the vasoconstrictor effect. Low $SjvO_2$ values could also suggest an increased demand for oxygen which may occur as a result of hyperthermia or shivering which increase oxygen consumption. Conversely, jugular venous saturation values above 75% may occur as a result of increased cerebral blood flow and mean arterial pressure following endotracheal suctioning. They may also suggest reduced oxygen extraction that may develop as a result of oversedation or, more worryingly, due to tentorial herniation causing brain stem compression and brain death.

There have been reported difficulties within the clinical setting using jugular venous saturation monitoring. Some authors note that falls in jugular venous saturation can lag behind increases in ICP while, in fact, obvious clinical deterioration had taken place before a fall in jugular venous oxygen saturation had taken place. (Sheinberg *et al*, 1992; Fortune *et al*, 1994). Problems have also occurred due to malposition or movement of the catheter, which can alter light intensity readings.

Non-invasive cerebral optical spectroscopy

Cerebral oxygenation can also be established by the use of a non invasive technique that employs similar principals to the more conventional pulse oximetry techniques commonly found in most wards and departments that measure systemic arterial oxygenation. A near infrared light source and two photodetectors are placed spatially apart on the temporal or parietal area of the scalp. Infrared light using a fibreoptic light source is transmitted through the scalp, partially absorbed by oxygenated and deoxygenated haemoglobin and reflected back to the two photodetectors. A computer within an oximeter calculates a regional cerebral oxygen saturation (Harris and Bailey, 1993; Mead *et al*, 1995; McCormick *et al*, 1991; Slavin *et al*, 1994; Germon, 1994; Williams *et al*, 1994b; Tateishi *et al*, 1995).

One of the major advantages of this monitoring method is that as a non-invasive, portable method of monitoring it is safe and easy to use in the clinical area. It obviously contributes to the understanding and recognition of altered cerebral haemodynamics in head injury. It also allows continuous monitoring of patients where it can detect inadequate oxygenation due to altered cerebral blood flow. Early interventions can therefore be initiated before there are obvious clinical signs of cerebral hypoxia and ischaemia. However, there are still many questions being raised into its use. Firstly, it has been demonstrated that in patients with anaemia, subdural haematomas or air collections between brain and scalp, low readings have been found. This is thought to be due to the scattering of light and not a fall in oxygen saturation (Slavin *et al*, 1994). It has also been argued that little is known about the effects on the signal that occur as a result of absorption of light by haemoglobin in superficial extracranial structures (Germon *et al*, 1994; Tateishi *et al*, 1995).

Electroencephalogram (EEG) monitoring

The measurement of brain electrical activity has been used in the diagnosis and management of conditions such as epilepsy and epileptiform activity as a result of acute and chronic focal lesions. Serial measurements can also be performed in patients with a wide variety of neurological dysfunctions to estimate improvement or failure of instigated treatment.

Table 4.5 lists the components of the EEG that are analysed.

Continuous computerised EEG recordings are being used more frequently in the monitoring of patients who have serious head injury or stroke within the intensive care unit. Proponents of its use indicate that EEG changes can be observed within seconds when there is a fall in cerebral blood flow due to intracranial hypertension or ischemia caused by cerebral vasoconstriction. The EEG can therefore assist in early recognition of neurological dysfunction and early treatment (Buzea, 1995). EEG changes occur when cerebral blood flow falls below 25ml/100 mg/min. Computerised EEG monitoring may also be used on a patient receiving thiopentone which is used to reduce cerebral metabolic rate in severe head injury. The aim is to reduce activity until 'burst suppression' occurs, thiopentone is then titrated to the EEG pattern achieved, overdose would result in overly long suppression (Buzea, 1995)

Table 4.5: EEG monitoring

Variable	Units of measurement	Comment
Frequency	Hertz	Divided into 4 bands; delta, theta (slow wave cycles), alpha and the fast activity band, beta
Amplitude	Microvolts per sencond	Measures height of wave
Symmetry	International standard set to determine electrode placement	Patterns of both hemispheres are compared
Reactivity		Alterations in activity as a result of noxious or verbal stimulation

However, there are a number of factors that can also influence the EEG pattern recorded and these must be considered while monitoring. Temperature changes, the effects of metabolic abnormalities together with drug administration can all influence the recording. (Miller *et al*, 1994).

Managing the priorities of patient care

The overall aim for management of patients who have received a serious cerebral insult is to maintain perfusion which reduce chances of secondary damage from oedema or ischaemia cause by reduced cerebral blood flow and oxygen delivery.

This section will deal with a number of strategies/ concerns that must be considered and are summarised in tables at the beginning of each subsection.

Ventilation

Table 4.6: Monitoring respiratory parameters

Priority	Management/intervention
• optimal ventilation to promote oxygenation and prevent cerebral vasoconstriction/ dilation	• maintain oxygen delivery • reduce oxygen consumption • hyperventilation to reduce cerebral blood flow • endotracheal suctioning

Maintaining oxygen supply and delivery to the unconscious patient may require the insertion of an endotracheal tube and the initiation of ventilatory support. Indeed, severely head injured patients receive this line of therapy in most neurosurgical intensive care units, rather than waiting until oxygen delivery becomes a problem. Another major reason for the initiation of artificial ventilation is to control a rising intracerebral pressure by managing the patients PCO_2. Cerebral blood vessels are very responsive to levels of carbon dioxide. Hypercapnia will cause cerebral vasodilation which will subsequently increase cerebral blood volume. This will increase ICP. Increased ICP will reduce CPP, causing a cerebral acidosis and eventually cerebral ischemia and neuronal death. It has generally been thought that creating a hypocarbic state will induce vasoconstriction, reduce cerebral blood flow and correct acidosis. Blood from high flow areas will be shunted to those areas that are poorly perfused. Patients have therefore been traditionally hyperventilated to reduce PCO_2 to lower than normal levels (25–30 mmHg). pH will also rise which assists in the mopping up of free radicals produced by damaged nerve cells. It is also customary practice in many neurosurgical units for patients to be hyperventilated by hand should ICP suddenly rise above 20–30 mmHg. Rapid 'hand bagging' is discontinued once the ICP reaches its base line level. However, while hyperventilation has been the first line management of patients with increased intracerebral pressure for some time, its use has been questioned (Geraci and Geraci, 1996a,b). A consistent problem in research studies that were reviewed by Geraci and Geraci (1996b) were that no consistent guidelines appear to be in place that would assist in the understanding of when lowered carbon dioxide levels become no longer therapeutic but become harmful. Intense vasoconstriction will cause cerebral ischaemia and so cause secondary damage rather than its prevention. Hand hyperventilation may also increase PEEP and intrathoracic pressure as the patient is given little time for exhalation. As a result, venous return from the head will fall causing an increase in cerebral blood volume, as well as a drop in cardiac output. Geraci and Geraci's review of the research also seemed to find that hyperventilation was associated with reduced arterial and jugular venous oxygen saturation and a poorer outcome. While these practices may still be evident in many intensive care units there is a trend towards managing patients with a PCO that is at the lower end of normal rather than the excessively low values of the past. However there does seem to be a deficit of standardised guidelines into the needs and use of hyperventilation by hand.

Artificial ventilation may also be required to improve oxygenation as the patient may have received serious chest trauma or have other pulmonary complications. Intermittent positive pressure ventilation with the use of PEEP will increase intrathoracic pressure. Raised intrathoracic pressures will reduce venous return from the head resulting in an increased cerebral blood volume.

Patients who are receiving ventilatory support will also require respiratory care. This involves the practice of endotracheal suctioning to ensure that pulmonary secretions are cleared and prevent the development of a hypostatic pneumonia. Some nursing researchers have focused on the effects endotracheal suctioning have had on intracranial pressure (Snyder, 1983; Crosby and Parsons, 1992; Brucia and Rudy, 1996; Rising, 1993). It is frequently observed in clinical practice that ICP rises during and after suctioning. A technique that produces the minimal rise has therefore been sought. Recommendations include; 2 suction passes per procedure and a minimum of a 10 minute rest period following suctioning to ensure that ICP and MAP can return to base line level. The use of hyperoxygenation prior to suctioning has also been explored. It has been thought that the rise in ICP is due to hypoxia which will transiently occur during suctioning. Hyperoxygenation could therefore prevent the hypoxic event and so minimise the rise in ICP. However, research has failed to demonstrate that hyper-oxygenation prior to suctioning will prevent a rise in ICP (Rudy *et al*, 1991; Rising, 1993; Brucia and Rudy, 1996). Recent work now suggests that receptors located in the carina may detect the movement of the tube during suctioning which then initiates a cerebrovascular and systemic response which causes the observed rise in ICP. Hypoxia and hypercapnia may not be the trigger at all (Rudy and Brucia, 1996).

Management of the circulation

Table 4.7: Managing the circulation

Priority	Management/intervention
Maintain cerebral circulation	• fluid and electrolyte management • drug management • nutritional management

The neural and renal systems, through a variety of feedback loops, finely control fluid and chemical balance. However, normal volume regulation is also controlled by the semi-permeable blood brain barrier. The blood brain barrier is the term used to describe the cerebral capillaries which have very different exchange rates and abilities to those capillaries found in other capillary beds. Crystalloid and osmotic pressure differences control transcapillary fluid transfer but only water, carbon dioxide and oxygen molecules pass through these capillary membranes with ease. Other molecules such as electrolytes pass through at very slow rates of exchange. The blood brain barrier is thought to be a protective mechanism that ensures a constant environment for nerve cells that would malfunction at even very small changes in the fluid and ionic balance (Ganong, 1985). Any neurological disturbance that damages the homeostatic systems or disrupts the blood brain barrier can cause fluid and electrolyte shifts, which may result in the development of cerebral oedema. Three different types of cerebral oedema have been identified in post traumatic injury. Vasogenic oedema, or an increase in extracellular fluid is commonly found in patients who have developed oedema as a result of trauma. Plasma molecules that are normally prevented from crossing the capillary membrane or blood brain barrier enter the extracellular space, osmotic pressure increases in the space which attract water molecules and promote oedema formation. Cytotoxic oedema, an increase in intracellular volume, will form if the sodium-potassium pumps on the cell membrane are disrupted. Water and sodium accumulate inside the cell disrupting cellular function and leading to ischaemia. This form of oedema may form as a result of cardiac arrest resuscitation, near drowning or some major hypoxic event. The third type of oedema, interstitial oedema is caused by an increase in sodium and water in the white matter surrounding the ventricles which interferes with CSF transport across the ventricular walls (Jacobs, 1995; Specht, 1995).

Traditional management of raised intracranial pressure usually involves reducing the volume of one or more of three intracranial components. Intracerebral blood volume can be reduced by inducing vasoconstriction through hyperventilation as described in the last section. Cerebrospinal fluid (CSF) volume can be reduced by the insertion of a ventricular drain and draining off CSF. Finally, the reduction of brain water can be accomplished by administering diuretics and fluid restriction (Asgeirsson *et al*, 1994).

Fluid replacement using crystalloid and colloids has traditionally been restricted to about 15–25 mls/Kg per day. This was thought to reduce the chances of increasing or developing cerebral oedema. However, it is now argued that inducing dehydration may contribute to poor renal function and a low blood pressure and therefore a low cerebral perfusion pressure. Fluid replacement is now administered to maintain normal physiological values.

Asgeirsson *et al* (1994) have proposed a different method of managing fluid volume. They argue that following damage to the blood brain barrier the osmotic pressure differences that usually control interstitial volume are less effective. The ideal therapy would be to treat the damaged blood brain barrier rather than controlling the fluid flux. Their work has centred on the use of a precapillary vasoconstrictor — dihydroergotamine, to decrease ICP by reducing cerebral blood volume. A hypotensive agent — metoprolol and clonidine, which do not act by vasodilation, is used, as it is suggested that by lowering arterial pressure there will be a reduction in transcapillary filtration across the damaged blood brain barrier.This therapy is maintained for about 7 days until the BBB has recovered. Albumin and blood transfusions were given to replace fluid losses. Managing cerebral oedema and intracranial pressure in this way is still not clinically widespread, but illustrates how the problem may be tackled in a very different way.

Attention has also focused on the use of indomethacin which is a prostoglandin inhibitor. A study by Biestro *et al* (1995) found that the use of indomethacin as an infusion was very effective in lowering ICP and improving CPP due to its vasoactive properties.

Mannitol, an osmotic diuretic, is frequently used to promote osmotic absorption of fluid from the extracelluar compartment into blood vessels which is then excreted by the kidneys. If the blood brain barrier is disrupted though these molecules may also pass into the interstitium and promote the uptake of more water through damaged cell membranes causing further oedema. This is known as the rebound effect.

The hypothalamus also plays a major role in maintaining fluid balance. Osmoreceptors located in the hypothalamus monitor osmolality of body fluid. If fluid levels decrease or solute levels increase, osmolality increases. The osmoreceptors will then trigger the thirst centre in the hypothalamus to initiate oral intake of fluid. The hypothalamus also produces antidiuretic hormone (ADH), which is stored in the pituitary gland. ADH acts on the renal tubules by making them more permeable to water. As osmolality increases, antidiuretic hormone is released and water is retained. Cerebral trauma that disrupts the pathways to the hypothalamus and pituitary may also disrupt these fluid volume control mechanisms. The following table summarises the causes, diagnosis and management (Parobek and Alaimo, 1996).

Table 4.8: Diagnosis and management of damage to fluid volume control mechanisms

	Diabetes insipidus	Syndrome of inappropriate antidiuretic hormone
Cause	Damage to supraoptic hypophysealportal pathway from trauma, neurosurgery or inflammation	Injury to hypothalamic neurohypophyseal system caused by brain tumour, abscess, trauma, bleed or meningitis
Serum sodium level	Greater than normal	Lower than normal
Urine sodium level	Low in relation to serum	Elevated
Urine specific gravity	<1.005	>1.005
Serum osmolality	Hyperosmolar	<280/Osm/L
Treatment	Fluid replenish	Fluid restriction IV sodium replacement
Diagnosis	Urine output >200mls for 2 consecutive hours Blood and urine chemistry	Blood chemistry Concentrated urine

(Adapted from Parobek and Alaimo, 1996)

Management of diabetes insipidus, which is commonly seen in patients with severe cerebral trauma and raised intracranial pressure, usually involves the use of pitressin or DDAVP.

Maintaining fluid volume also involves the provision of nutritional support. Lack of adequate nutrition in neurotrauma patients has been associated with a prolonged recovery, translocation of bacteria causing sepsis and a poor outcome, as it does in any group of patients who are critically ill. As a result early (within 48 hours) enteral feeding has been promoted in most critical care areas. Research into whether early nutrition can improve rehabilitation outcome and reduce the incidence of complications in the severe head injured patient is being conducted (Taylor and Fettes, unpublished; Stechmiller *et al*, 1994). However, issues relating to nutrition of the critically ill patient are discussed in another chapter.

Managing the circulation of the patient with a cerebral bleed

Fluid management in patients who have had a cerebral bleed is directed at increasing cerebral perfusion and cerebral blood flow in order to overcome vasospasm and reduce the risk of ischaemia. In order to achieve hyperperfusion, therapy that includes volume expansion, arterial hypertension and haemodilution using crystalloids and colloids is used. This approach will improve the cerebral microcirculation and decrease blood viscosity. Increased arterial pressure can be achieved by using vasoconstrictor agents such as metaraminol (aramine) which are titrated to increase mean arterial pressure to above 70mmHg. Continuous neurological assessment is required as the major complication is fluid overload, which may cause raised ICP, pulmonary oedema and further rebleeding (Rusy, 1996).

Treatment may also include the use of the calcium channel blocker, nimodipine, which has an affinity for cerebral vessels. It blocks the influx of calcium which reduces smooth muscle spasm.

Surgical management of this group would include the evacuation of the haematoma if necessary and clipping of the aneurysm. In recent years treatment has included the insertion of platinum coils. The coil is soldered onto a catheter tip and inserted into the aneurysm. Once released into the aneurysm the coil conforms to the shape of the aneurysmal sac forming a graft (Coleman and Sifri-Steele, 1994).

While these therapies have improved outcome, death and disability still occur as a result of the damage caused by the bleed and the effects of vasospasm. Attention is now being focused on the use of thrombolytics, such as tissue plasminogen activator, to promote early clot dissolution (Bell and Kongable, 1996). Vasoactive mediators that are released from the clot as it degrades are thought to mediate vasospasm, therefore early removal of the clot could reduce the incidence of spasm (Whitney, 1994; Macabasco and Hickman, 1995; Armstrong, 1994). A steroidal compound that is an inhibitor of free radical-mediated lipid perioxidation, a process that is thought to induce spasm, is also the centre of some clinical trials (Rusy, 1996).

Managing thermoregulation

Priority	Intervention/management
Thermoregulatory imbalance	• continuous temperature monitoring • cooling central fever • induced hypothermia

Thermoregulatory control occurs within the preoptic region of the hypothalamus. Mechanisms that initiate vaso-constriction and vasodilation, sweating and piloerection are initiated in response to the hypothalamus triggering the production of hormones in the adrenals, pituitary and thyroid. The hypothalamus will also initiate the cortex to adopt a number of behaviourial mechanisms that will either promote heat gain or loss. Disruption to the neural networks that control the body's temperature can induce 'central fever'. The temperature can become elevated in response to compression or trauma and is often not accompanied with infection. It is thought that the mechanism behind this may be due to Interleukin 1 (IL-1), a cytokine released by the immune system in response to the trauma (Holtzclaus, 1992; Segatore, 1992). IL-1 may promote the production prostoglandin, a fever inducing substance, by acting on a number of biochemical pathways. Whatever the cause of the fever in neurotrauma, it is metabolically costly. Oxygen consumption and carbon dioxide production rises when temperature is elevated and shivering is initiated. Cerebral blood volume will also rise which will increase ICP. Management of central fever has been the focus of a number of studies which have considered the effects of drugs (Meythaler and Stinton, 1994; Segatore, 1992). However, another important facet of temperature control in neurotrauma has been the use of active cooling of body temperature below normal that has regained interest in neurotrauma centres. Therapeutic prolonged moderate hypothermia (28–32°C) was introduced in the resuscitation of cerebral trauma in the 1950s to reduce ICP. Patients were cooled using drugs such as thiopentone, paralysing agents or 'lytic cocktail' (pethedine, chlorpromazine and promethazine), the action of the drugs prevented shivering as the patients temperature fell (Rosmoff *et al*, 1996). Rosmoff *et al* also report that complications such as pneumonia and coagulation problems did not appear to be problematic despite hypothermia being maintained for up to six weeks. However in some patients, ICP rose on rewarming causing brain herniation and it was also reported by other centres that management of prolonged hypothermia did present clinical problems and outcome results were not convincing. The practice was therefore almost abandoned (Shiozaki *et al*, 1993). In the last decade mild hypothermia (34–35°C) as a means of controlling intracranial pressure has been reintroduced. Studies by Marion *et al* (1993) and Shiozaki *et al* (1993) have produced results that suggest this form of management is a safe and effective method of controlling cerebral hypertension and that outcome is improved.

Sedation

Patients who have sustained a severe cerebral insult may require intubation and ventilation to firstly manage their airway and oxygenation due to an inadequate respiratory drive, but also to hyperventilate to induce hypocapnia. In order to make this procedure comfortable for the patient and to ensure patient compliance, sedative drugs may be required. Some patients do not respond to the traditional methods of controlling ICP, ie. hyperventilation, fluid restriction and CSF drainage and so may require the use of sedation and muscle relaxants to control ICP (McLelland *et al*, 1995). The use of this drug combination does have inherent difficulties as neurological assessment that involves the assessment of cognition and motor response will not be possible. The effects of muscle relaxants can also be far reaching causing reduced gastric motility and delayed nutritional delivery. The pupil may also become difficult to assess if opiates or barbiturates are used to sedate, although the pupil will usually fix and dilate if herniation occurs.

Similar difficulties are encountered during the use of thiopentone. Thiopentone was used considerably for the control of a rapid rising intracranial pressure in the 1970s and early 1980s. However, the drug has a very long half life making it very difficult to assess the patient even following its discontinuation. Medical studies also appeared to suggest that outcome did not necessarily improve. Nevertheless the drug is still used today in those patients who have not responded to a variety of therapies and have sustained cerebral hypertension (Mirski *et al*, 1995).

Managing noxious stimuli

Auditory stimuli

Two areas within the temporal lobe are associated with auditory function. Connections between the two as well as connections to other parts of the cortex are necessary in order to process and interpret sound. Damage to these areas or brain swelling would make it difficult for the patient to be able to interpret sound or understand conversation. It may therefore be difficult to establish whether the familiar sound of conversation from friends and family may be reassuring to the patient or cause distress due to an inability to process the content or familiarity of the conversation. Some nursing research has focused on the effects of conversation on ICP (Johnstone *et al,* 1989; Treolar *et al*, 1991). Schinner *et al* (1995) used music,silence and ICU environmental noise as auditory stimuli and examined the effect on ICP and CPP. However, little conclusive evidence about its benefit or the generation of a physiologic response appears to have been determined.

Nursing care activities

It is frequently observed in clinical practice that ICP rises sharply in response to nursing care activities. This may already be in the presence of a sustained elevated ICP, therefore the further rise would be cause for concern. Nursing research has therefore considered which care activities cause the sharp rise and how these essential acts of care, such as repositioning, oral hygiene and bedbathing, could be continued without causing serious harm to the patient. A wide variation of response in ICP has been reported by some authors following repositioning and head elevation (March *et al,* 1990; Rising, 1993; Jones, 1995). Other activities such as bedbathing and oral hygiene can also produce a varied response (Rising, 1993; Hugo, 1987). It has also been postulated that spacing activities apart from allowing rest periods between activities could reduce sustained rises in ICP. However most appear to agree that the extent of the response would depend on the extent to which autoregulation of cerebral blood flow had been lost. The recommendations drawn from the research all suggest that individualised assessment of the patients response to care activities is necessary as the responses shown were highly individualised in nature.

Nevertheless, ICP can be managed by keeping the head in alignment with the shoulders which prevents kinking of the jugular vein and promote good venous return and CSF circulation.

Conclusion

The patient who has received a major neurological insult as a result of trauma or a cerebral bleed may be admitted to any general intensive care unit. Many of these patients may be referred on to a neurological centre for specialist intervention and management. However the first few hours are crucial and require careful assessment and management to prevent secondary damage and so improve outcome. Nevertheless standard guidelines that recognise research findings and recommendations appear to be lacking. A telephone survey in 1996 (Jeevaratnam and Menon, 1996) of intensive care management for head injured patients in the United Kingdom revealed that practices varied considerably. Moderate hyperventilation, the use of corticosteroids (useful in managing cerebral tumours) and reliance on inappropriate assessment tools are still evident. The nurse who has been charged with the patient's care must therefore look to the research evidence to ensure that those areas of care that can be manipulated by the nurse, comply with the prevention of secondary damage. Furthermore, the nurse must develop skills in interpretation, recognition and evaluation as changes in cerebral functioning can change rapidly without warning.

References

Armstrong S (1994) Cerebral vasospasm: early detection and
    intervention. *Crit Care Nurse* **14**: 33–37
Asgeirsson B, Grande OO, Nordstrom CH (1994) A new therapy
    of post-trauma brain oedema based on haemodynamic
    principles for brain volume regulation. *Intensive Care Med*
    20: 260–267
Bell TE, Kongable GL (1996) Innovations in aneurysmal
    subarachnoid haemorrhage: intracisternal t-PA for the
    prevention of vasospasm. *J Neurosci Nurs* 28(2): 107–113
Biestro AA, Alberti RA, Cancela MA, Puppo CB, Borovitch B
    (1995) Use of indomethacin in brain injured patients with
    cerebral perfusion impairment: preliminary report. *J
    Neurosurg* **83**: 627–630
Brucia J, Rudy E (1996) The effect of suction catheter insertion
    and tracheal stimulation in adults with severe brain injury.
    Heart Lung 25(4): 295–303
Buzea CE (1995) Understanding computerized EEG monitoring
    in the intensive care unit. *J Neurosci Nurs* **27**(5): 292–297
Coleman R, Sifri-Steele C (1994) Treatment of posterior
    circulation aneurysms using platinum coils. *J Neurosci Nurs*
    26(6): 367–370
Crosby LJ, Parsons LC (1992) Cerebrovascular response of closed
    head injuries to a standardised endotracheal tube suctioning
    and manual hyperventilation procedure. *J Neurosci Nurs*
    24(1): 40–49
Cruz J, Miner ME, Allen SJ *et al* (1991) Continuous monitoring
    of cerebral oxygenation in acute brain injury: assessment of
    cerebral haemodynamic reserve. *Neurosurgery* **29**(5):
    743–749
Eddy VA, Vitsky JL, Rutherford EJ *et al* (1995) Aggressive use of
    ICP monitoring is safe and alters patient care. *Am Surg*
    61(1): 24–29
Ellis A, Cavanagh SJ (1992) Aspects of neurosurgical assessment
    using the Glasgow coma scale. *Intensive Crit Care Nurs* **8**:
    94–99
Fearon M, Rusy KL (1994) Transcranial doppler: advanced
    technology for assessing cerebral haemodynamics.
    Dimensions Crit Care Nurs **13**(5): 241–248
Fielding K, Rowley G (1990) Reliability of assessments by skilled
    observers using the Glasgow coma scale. *Aust J Advanced
    Nurs* **7**(4): 13–17
Fortune JB, Feustral PJ, Weigle GM, Popp AJ (1994) Continuous
    measurement of jugular venous oxygen saturation in
    response to transient elevations of blood pressure in
    head-injured patients. *J Neurosurg* **80**: 461–468
Ganong WF (1985) *Review of Medical Physiology, Twelfth
    Edition*. Lange Medical Publications, Los Altos
Geraci EB, Geraci TA (1996a) Hyperventilation and head injury:

controversies and concerns. *J Neurosci Nurs* **28**(4): 381–387

Geraci E, Geraci T (1996b) A look at recent hyperventilation studies: outcomes and recommendations for early use in the head-injured patient. *J Neurosci Nurs* **28**(4): 222–233

Germon TJ, Kane NM, Manara AR *et al* (1994) Near-infrared spectroscopy in adults: effects of extracranial ischaemia and intracranial hypoxia on estimation of cerebral oxygenation. *J Anaes* **73**: 503–506

Harris DNF, Bailey SM (1993) Near infrared spectroscopy in adults. *Anaesthesia* **48**: 694–696

Hickey JV (1992) *Neurological and Neurological Nursing* (3rd edn). JB Lippincott, Philadelphia

Holtzclaw BJ (1992) The febrile response in critical care: State of the science. *Heart Lung* **21**(5): 482–501

Hugo M (1987) Alleviating the effects of care on the intracranial pressure (ICP) of head-injured patients by manipulating nursing care activities. *Intensive Care Nurs* **3**:78–82

Ingersoll GL, Leyden DB (1987) The Glasgow coma scale for patients with head injuries. *Crit Care Nurse* **7**(5): 26–32

Jacobs BB (1995) Emergent neurologic events. *Crit Care Nurs Clin North America* **7**(3): 427–444

Jeevaratnam DR, Menon DK (1996) Survey of intensive care for severely head-injured patients in the United Kingdom. *Br Med J* **312**: 944–947

Jennett B, Teasdale G (1984) *Management of Head Injuries*. FA DAVIS Company, Philadelphia

Johnson SM, Omery A, Nikas D (1989) Effects of conversation on intracranial pressure in comatose patients. *Heart Lung* **18** (1): 56–63

Jones B (1995) The effects of patient repositioning on intracranial pressure. *Aust J Advanced Nurs* **12**(2): 32–39

Juarez VJ, Lyons M (1995) Interrator Reliability of the Glasgow Coma Scale. *J Neurosci Nurs* **27**(5): 213–214

Kapadia F, Jha AN (1995) Monitoring and management of raised intracranial pressure (ICP) in the intensive care unit with an analysis of one year of intracranial pressure monitoring. *J Associated Physicians India* **43**(11): 783–790

Kirkpatrick PJ, Smielewski P, Czosnyka M *et al* (1994) Continuous monitoring of cortical perfusion by laser doppler flowmetry in ventilated patients with head injury. *J Neurol Neurosurg Psychiatry* 57: 1382–1388

Lucke KT, Kerr ME, Chovanes GI (1995) Continuous bedside cerebral blood flow monitoring. *J Neurosci Nurs* **27**(2): 72–77

Macabasca AC, Hickman JL (1995) Thrombolytic therapy for brain attack. *J Neurosci Nurs* **27**(3): 138–149

March K, Mitchell P, Grady S *et al* (1990) Effect of backrest position on intracranial and cerebral perfusion pressures. *J Neurosci Nurs* **22**(6): 375–381

Marion DW, Obrist WD, Carlier PM *et al* (1993) The use of moderate hypothermia for patients with severe head injuries: a preliminary report. *J Neurosurg* **79**: 354–362

Mead GE, Williams IM, McCollum CN *et al*(1995) Near infrared cerebral spectroscopy. A method for continuous measurement of cerebral oxygenation. *Br J Intensive Care* **5**(6): 194–199

Meythaler J, Stinton AM (1994) Fever of central origin in traumatic brain injury controlled with propanalol arch. *Phys Rehabilitation* July, **75**: 816–818

McLelland M, Woster P, Sweasey T *et al* (1995) Continuous midazolam/ atracurium infusions for the management of increased intracranial pressure. *J Neurosci Nurs* **27**(2): 96–101

McCormick PW, Stewart M, Goetting MG *et al* (1991) Non-invasive cerebral optical spectroscopy for monitoring cerebral oxygen delivery and haemodynamics. *Crit Care Med* 19(1): 89–97

Miller JD, Piper IR, Jones PA (1994) Integrated multimodality monitoring in the neurosurgical intensive care unit. *Neurosurg Clin N Am* **5**(4): 661–670

Mirski MA, Muffelman B, Ulatowski JA *et al* (1995) Sedation for the critically ill neurologic patient. *Crit Care Med* **23**(12): 2038–2053

Parobek V, Alaimo I (1996) Fluid and electrolyte management in the neurologically impaired patient. *J Neurosci Nurs* **28**(5): 322–328

Pollack-Latham C (1987) Intracranial pressure monitoring: Part 1. physiologic principles. *Crit Care Nurse* **7**(5): 40–51

Price TE (1996) An evaluation of neuro-assessment tools in the intensive care unit. *Nurs Crit Care* **1**(2): 72–77

Prociuk JL (1995) Management of cerebral oxygen supply-demand balance in blunt head injury. *Crit Care Nurse* August: 38–44

Rising CJ (1993) The Relationship of Selected Nursing Activities to ICP. *J Neurosci Nurs* **25**(5): 302–308

Robinson S (1992) The Glasgow coma scale: a critical look. *Axon* September: 21–23

Rosmoff HL, Kochanek PM, Clark R *et al* (1996) Resuscitation from severe brain trauma. *Crit Care Med* **24**(2) (Suppl)

Rudy EB, Turner BS, Baun M *et al* (1991) Endotracheal suctioning in adults with head injury. *Heart Lung* **20**(6): 667–674

Rusy KL (1996) Rebleeding and Vasospasm after Subarachnoid Haemorrhage. *Crit Care Nurse* **16**(1): 41–47

Segatore M, Way C (1992) The Glasgow coma scale: time for change. *Heart Lung* **21**(6): 548–556

Segatore M (1992) Fever after traumatic brain injury. *J Neurosci Nurs* **24**(2): 104–109

Schinner KM, Chisolm AH, Grap MJ *et al* (1995) Effects of auditory stimuli on intracranial pressure and cerebral perfusion pressure in traumatic brain injury. *J Neurosci Nurs* **27**(6): 348–354

Sheinberg M, Kanter MJ, Robertson CS *et al* (1992) Continuous monitoring of jugular venous oxygen saturation in head injured patients. *J Neurosurg* **76**: 212–217

Shiozaki T, Sugimoto H, Taneda M *et al* (1993) Effect of mild hypothermia on uncontrollable intracranial hypertension after severe head injury. *J Neurosurg* **79**: 363–368

Slavin KV, Dujovny M, Ausman JI *et al* (1994) Clinical experience with transcranial cerebral oximetry. *Surg Neurol* **42**: 531–540

Snyder M (1983) Relation of nursing activities to increases in intracranial pressure. *J Adv Nurs* **8**: 273–279

Specht DM (1995) Cerebral Edema. *Nursing* November: 34–38

Stechmiller J, Treolar DM, Derrico D *et al* (1994) Interruption of enteral feedings in head injured patients. *J Neurosci Nurs* **26**(4): 224–229

Tateishi A, Maekawa T, Soejimma Y *et al* (1995) Qualitative comparison of carbon dioxide-induced change in cerebral near-infrared spectroscopy versus jugular venous oxygen saturation in adults with acute brain disease. *Crit Care Med* **23**(10): 1734–1738

Teasdale G, Jennett B (1974) Assessment of coma and impaired consciousness. *Lancet* July 13: 81–83

Teasdale G (1975) Assessing 'conscious level'. *Nurs Times* June 12

Treolar DM, Jermier Nalli B, Guin P *et al* (1991) The effect of familiar and unfamiliar voice treatments on intracranial pressure in head injured patients. *J Neurosci Nurs* **23**(5): 295–299

Whitney F. (1994) Drug therapy for acute stroke. *J Neurosci Nurs* **26**(2): 111–117

Williams IM, Picton A, Farrell GE *et al* (1994a) Light-reflective cerebral oximetry and jugular bulb venous oxygen during carotid endarterectomy. *J Surg* **81**:1291–1295

Williams IM, Picton AJ, Hardy SC *et al* (1994b) Cerebral hypoxia detected by near infrared spectroscopy. *Anaesth* **49**: 762–766

5

Managing the nutritional priorities in the critically ill patient

Introduction

The objectives of this chapter are:
- to discuss effective strategies for assessing nutritional requirements in the critically ill
- to discuss the priorities of care when administering enteral nutrition to the critically ill
- to discuss potential complications that may occur.

The physiology of metabolism and nutritional requirements both in health and disease are well documented as are the complications of parental feeding and so will not be discussed within this chapter. The need to initiate feeding is an aspect of care that may be neglected in the early hours of a patient's admission to an intensive care unit. Assessing, monitoring and evaluating the interventions required to stabilise a patient with a life-threatening condition take precedence. However, it would now appear that the gut, far from being quiescent during this period of physiological instability, has an important role to play in the prevention of sepsis. It is also recognised that loss of autoregulation of blood supply to the gut can result in the gut mucosal cells breaking down allowing the translocation of bacteria. This can potentiate another life threatening condition — sepsis.

The critical care nurse may be the first person to consider the need for feeding a patient admitted to the intensive care unit. . There has also been a growth of interest in issues surrounding the provision of enteral feeding which perhaps need reviewing to seek clarification. This chapter considers the literature on enteral feeding in an attempt to clarify the pertinent issues which may be of concern when planning to enterally feed the critically ill patient in intensive care.

Definitions

The role of the gut

The digestive tract, in health, breaks down foodstuffs by mechanical and chemical activities. These products are then reprocessed and transported to cells for energy use, storage or the formulation of new cells and structures (digestion and absorption). The tract also plays an important role in the defence against infection. The mucosa of the gut forms a protective barrier between the 'sterile interior' and 'gut lumen'. The gut mucosal cells undergo continuous proliferation and so require an adequate supply of blood. During periods of hypoperfusion, for example, in serious stress induced situations, hypovolaemia, sepsis and trauma, the cells degenerate. Tight junctions between the cells open up and allow bacteria to translocate from the gut lumen into the systemic blood supply. The gut may also be heavily colonised with bacteria during periods of serious illness or antibiotic use thereby increasing the risk of transfer of bacteria (Keithley and Eisenberg, 1993). Maintenance of gut integrity is therefore being increasingly recognised as important in the prevention of sepsis and as an adjunct to the immune system defences.

Causative factors of malnourishment

Increased metabolic demands

Glucose is the primary energy substrate, however, in a state of increased metabolic activity stores of glucose in skeletal muscle and the liver are used up within twenty four hours. If activity increases and demand continues, glucose is then produced from secondary substrates, that is, protein and fats. This process is known as gluconeogensis. Patients in intensive care have either a serious illness due to disease or trauma, which may lead to an increased demand for energy. Fever will also increase the basal metabolic rate as will infection and tissue repair processes (Holmes, 1987).

Malnutrition can occur when there is a deficit of nutrients required to maintain bodily processes (Verity, 1996). McWhirter and Pennington (1994) report that in a survey of 500 hospital patients, 40% were undernourished and 5.4% lost

Table 5.1: Effects of starvation

System	Effect
Immune	Immunosuppression causing:
	• infection
	• pressure sores
	• colonisation of bacteria
	• impaired wound healing
Motor	• skeletal muscle atrophy
	• reduced mobility
	• respiratory muscle weakness leading to inadequate alveolar ventilation, so unable to excrete carbon dioxide
Respiratory	• nosocomial lung infection
	• ventilator dependency
Reduced autoregulation of blood flow in gut	• mucosal cell wall atrophy
	• translocation of bacteria
Reduced plasma proteins	• peripheral and pulmonary oedema
Psychological disturbance	• poor concentration
	• anxious, apathetic or depressed
(Taylor and Goodinson-McLaren, 1992; Keithley and Eisenberg, 1993; Verity, 1996)	

weight during their hospital stay which suggests that the achievement of balancing demand with supply is not being met. It has also been shown that eventual outcome from serious illness can be influenced by the nutritional status. As a result, nutritional support has become an integral part of critical care (Berger and Adams, 1989).

Protein energy malnutrition is the most common form of malnutrition seen in Britain. It can develop as a result of being exposed to a continuous stressor, such as critical illness. Increased metabolism due to fever or trauma, or malabsorption and poor utilisation of nutrients are all factors that contribute to protein energy deficiency (Taylor and Goodinson-McLaren, 1992; Horwood, 1990). *Table 5.1* illustrates the many differing effects that starvation may have.

Assessment of priorities of care

Obtaining a history

All patients in the critical care area need a nutritional assessment that evaluates both their current state of nourishment and their nutritional needs.

Taylor and Goodinson-McLaren (1992) identify three main aims of nutritional assessment:

- to evaluate baseline parameters of nourishment status at a set point in time and obtain information on the adequacy of recent nutrient intake
- to identify individuals who require nutritional support
- to evaluate by serial measurement the efficacy of nutritional support.

The British Association of Parental and Enteral Nutrition (BAPEN) guidelines suggest that assessment should be performed within 48 hours of admission and outlines four questions that should be asked of the patient during this assessment (Silk, 1994). However, 48 hours post admission may be too late in the prevention of the breakdown of the gut mucosa lumen leading to the translocation of bacteria into the blood stream in the critically ill patient. The patient may also be seriously malnourished due to the presence of long term illness. Therefore the patient should be assessed as soon as possible after admission. The information from questions such as; 'Have you unintentionally lost weight recently?' or 'Have you been eating less than usual?' as outlined by BAPEN (Norton, 1996), may be difficult to obtain from the patient who has been admitted as an emergency to the intensive care unit. Reilly *et al* (1987) outline a number of at risk criteria that can assist the intensive care nurse to establish whether the patient has been malnourished before admission or is at risk now. Factors such as a history obtained from relatives or ward staff of a reduced dietary intake as a result of a lowered conscious level, or prolonged fasting for major surgery or procedures would be important factors to consider. Similarly, diarrhoea, vomiting or protein loss from wounds or burns would contribute to a malnourished state.

Scanlon *et al* (1994) devised an assessment tool that

was based on the same principles as the Waterlow Pressure Sore Prevention and Treatment System (cited by Scanlon *et al*, 1994). They found that previously identified assessment tools were time-consuming and difficult to use. Seven criteria were identified from considering Butterworth's work (cited by Scanlon *et al*, 1994) who had identified eight factors that contribute to iatrogenic malnourishment. Each category is further subdivided and scored, and checked against a nursing action plan. This therefore assists the nurse in identifying the patient who is nutritionally at risk and monitoring subsequent nutritional support.

Anthropometric measurements and predicator tables

Nutritional anthropometry involves the measurement of body weight, height, skinfold thickness and limb muscle circumference and areas. Serial measurements of these parameters can be used to calculate changes in protein mass and the body's energy stores. The patient's body mass index (BMI) may also be used to calculate the patients nutritional status. This index is calculated from the patient's weight and height (BMI= wt kg/ht m_2). Nomograms can assist in the calculation and provide some information about normal limits. However, it can be difficult to measure the patients weight in the intensive care unit, particularly if there is no weight bed available, or the patient has weighty incumbrances such as traction, plaster of Paris splints or gross oedema as a result of trauma. Estimates of weight are commonly used or by obtaining the information from knowledgable relatives! Nevertheless, while this may give a baseline it would be difficult to regularly estimate an accurate BMI in many critically ill patients (Endacott, 1993). Measurement of limb skin fold thickness can provide information about the distribution of subcutaneous fat distribution. Taylor and Goodinson-McLaren (1992) indicate that this measurement will not give an indication of total body fat but serial measurements can indicate whether fat is being used as an energy source. Measuring skinfold thickness is a skilled procedure and the measurement itself is prone to a number of variables. Subcutaneous fat distribution is known to vary considerably between ages, sexes, and ethnic groups. In the critically ill patient hydration status can vary considerably, oedema and dehydration can make the measurement unreliable (Taylor and Goodinson-McLaren, 1992).

Metabolic monitoring

Metabolic monitoring, which uses indirect calorimetry, is becoming a popular method of establishing oxygen consumption, carbon dioxide elimination and the respiratory quotient, in the intensive care unit. From this data, energy expenditure is calculated and calorie requirements determined. An open circuit metabolic monitor can be attached to the ventilator which samples inspiratory and expiratory O_2 and CO_2 providing a continuous measurement of energy expenditure (Adams, 1994). However metabolic monitoring does have limitations. Accuracy in the data provided decreases in patients who require oxygen concentrations greater than 60%, a factor that may limit its use in the sickest of patients. Haemofiltration and haemo-diafiltration will also facilitate the loss of carbon dioxide in solution, therefore exhaled carbon dioxide levels will be lower. The level measured at the metabolic monitor attached to the ventilator will therefore not reflect the level produced by metabolic activity (Adams, 1994).

Biochemical assessment

The concentration of biochemical markers in urine and plasma can provide information about the patient's nutritional status. Protein markers such as; albumen, transferrin, retinol binding protein and thyroxine binding prealbumen are all synthesised in the liver, their concentrations giving information on their rates of synthesis and utilisation (Goodinson, 1986). For example, declining concentrations in serum albumen could suggest chronic starvation. However, the critically ill patient may have excessive losses due to major wounds, fistulae or burns. In addition, fluxes between the intracellular and extracellular compartments due to a leaky vasculature can result in low serum albumin levels (Goodinson, 1986).

Table 5.2: Summary of assessment tools

Measurement	Advantages	Disadvantages
History using criteria	Relatively quick and easy to do. Early identification of problems. Tools incorporated into care plans enable regular monitoring and evaluation.	Unable to gain much information from taking history — so record is incomplete. Observation may be subjective and so unreliable.
Anthropometry: Body weight Body mass index	Changes in protein mass and the rate of change in energy stores can be estimated.	Requires the routine use of a weigh bed. May also be inaccurate due to gross oedema or external weights such as plaster of Paris or traction. Skilled technique which may require the same person to conduct the assessment each time in order to reduce error.
Skinfold thickness	Serial measurements can indicate whether fat is being used as an energy source.	Problems with accuracy due to differences in reference values for different age groups. Also the presence of hypoalbumin-aemia, alteration in glycogen content and impaired neurological function will reduce accuracy.
Skeletal muscle mass	Can indicate if protein is being used as a source.	
Biochemical: Serum protiens Nitrogen balance	Provides an indicator of protein catabolism.	Some tests are difficult to obtain. Standard values do not always assist in determining starvation in some individuals. Changes in fluid distribution can distort results.
Metabolic monitoring	Continuous measure-ment of energy expenditure and thus accurage calculation of calorie requirement can be calculated. Useful in the ventilated patient in intensive care.	Inaccurate in the patient who is receiving $>60\%$ O_2. Inaccurate in the patient who is receiving haemo/haemodialfiltration due to loss of dissolved CO_2 through the filter membrane.
Computerised axial tomography Nuclear magnetic resonance	Accurately estimate organ and tissue composition. Enables protein mass and fat and water distribution to be calculated.	Not available for routine nutritional assessment to be made. Expensive.

Assessment tools have been criticised by many authors for the time they take to perform and the detailed analysis required to obtain the relevant information. Tools such as anthropometric and biochemical measurements are time-consuming. Similarly, it has been shown that energy expenditure predictor formulae and tables are often inaccurate when used within the critically ill group of patients. Inaccuracy may be due to the effects of stress due to critical illness on the metabolic rate and hormonal response (Goodinson, 1986).

Managing the nutritional priorities of care

The advantages and disadvantages of total parental nutrition (TPN) versus enteral nutrition (EN) are well documented in the literature. Aseptic techniques in the maintenance of lines can reduce the incidence of line related septicaemia and feeding regimes using TPN are manipulated to reduce the incidence of hyperlipidaemia, hyperglycaemia. However, the nurses role in the critical care area is now more predominantly concerned with the use of enteral nutrition since it has been shown that early feeding can reduce the incidence of the translocation of bacteria into the blood stream and the development of septicaemia (Keithly and Eisenberg, 1993).

The priorities of care can be identified as:

• the gastric tube used to deliver the feed
• establishing the correct position of the enteral tube
• feeding regimes.

The gastric tube

Jones (1986), Bastow (1988), Field (1988) and Shaw (1994) have all documented a number of complications and problems that occur in the use of Ryles tubes for nasogastric feeding. Erosion, oesphagitis, gastric reflux, incompetent oeso- phageal sphincter, ulceration, stenosis or perforation have all been cited as occurring as a direct result of nasoenteric tube feeding. In order to prevent or reduce these complications many authors advocate the use of fine bore tubes but Briggs (1996) argues that research evidence to support the notion that there are less complications when using fine bore tubes is scanty. Briggs also indicates that data in support of the idea that large bore feeding tubes cause oesophageal damage is difficult to locate.

Reported complications in using fine bore tubes include; bronchial, peritoneal or intracranial placement causing, pneumonia, hydrothorax, emphysema (Metheny *et al*, 1990).

This may be due to several factors such as:

- difficulty with auscultation
- tube collapses during aspiration, therefore difficult to aspirate and check contents for pH. However, Metheny *et al* (1989) found that in 90% of attempts on a study group over a 14 month period sufficient fluid could be obtained for testing
- placement requires the use of a stylet.

Fine bore tubes therefore require X-rays to confirm their position. However, they are easily displaced, and can migrate into the respiratory tract without any obvious change in clinical signs such as increased coughing (Metheny *et al*, 1989). The critically ill patient though may be at risk if fine bore tubes are used. There is a need to assess frequently gastric residual volumes, as many drugs used in the intensive care environment can alter or slow gastric emptying. Therefore, in order to assess the volume of feed that the patient can tolerate regular assessment of the gastric residual volume is required. This practice may be difficult to ascertain when using a fine bore tube (Metheny, 1993). Secondly, slow gastric emptying and poor oesophageal sphincter control can also increase the risk of aspiration in the unconscious patient. Kacan and Hickisch (1986) also found in a study looking at feeding problems associated with the neurologically compromised patient that small bore feeding tubes did not preclude aspiration in two patients within their study group. A low pressure, high volume endotracheal cuff may not prevent gastric contents moving into the respiratory tract. Briggs (1996b) suggests a number of criteria that could be used in evaluating the best gastric tube to be used on the intensive care unit. Firstly, that it is suitable for long term use. Secondly, that the position of the tube can be checked through auscultation and aspiration. Thirdly, that the material from which it is made of allows a frequent check of gastric volume and lastly that insertion does not require a stylet. However, the nasoenteric route can be used to overcome these difficulties or indeed the placement of a feeding jejeunostomy tube.

Tube placement

Metheny has considered the efficacy of different methods of determining tube placement over a number of years. In a literature review (1993) she found that published research was not available to support the practice of assessing the visual characteristics of the aspirate to determine whether it is gastric in origin. Metheny (1993) points out that there are case study reports of fluid that had actually been aspirated from the respiratory tract that was mistaken for gastric content. It can be assumed that this could lead to feeding being continued into the respiratory tract. The presence of 'whooshing' or 'gurgling' noises in the stomach when air is insufflated into the tube is commonly used to ascertain placement of the tube. Metheny (1993) indicates in the review that a number of authors suggest that this noise will not be heard if the tube has been inadvertently placed in the respiratory tract. This claim, though, has been refuted by a number of sources. Metheny *et al* (1990) reports that in a study of nine patients who had inadvertently had tubes placed in the respiratory tree, all the physicians and nurses reported in all but one case that the sounds heard were consistent with the tube being situated in the stomach. Gastric pH is very acid with an approximate range of 1.5–5.5. Establishing that the aspirate is within this range would confirm to the nurse that the tube is in the correct place (Neill *et al*, 1993). However, Metheny also (1993) suggests that there is considerable variability in gastric pH and it may be affected by the presence of feed or the administration of H_2 antagonists. Indeed, the ageing process is thought to reduce acid secretion and the reflux of intestinal secretions due to the presence of pain or stress may also make the pH appear more alkaline. It is also known that patients who have an oesophageal rupture, empyema or respiratory malignancy may have acidic respiratory secretions (Metheny, 1993). Metheny *et al* (1989) suggests that while pH assessment can be used effectively in most patients, it should be delayed for one hour after feeding and that the tube should be flushed with 50 millilitres of air to clear it of any substances. A well recognised sign of respiratory placement of the tube is the observation of respiratory distress. The patient who is persistently coughing or choking with a deterioration in respiratory function would lead most to suspect that the tube has been misplaced. However, this is an unreliable indicator in the critically ill patient who may be sedated and ventilated, unconscious, or have a diminished gag reflex. It has also been reported that fine bore tubes may not initiate the cough reflex (Metheny *et al*, 1990). Further, respiratory function deterioration could also be attributed to other concurrent events. The presence of bubbles when the end of the tube is placed under water is thought by some authors to suggest that air is being expired from the respiratory tract and so suggest respiratory placement. Case study reports, again cited by Metheny, suggest that this too is an unreliable method. The most effective method would appear to be X-ray confirmation. Fortunately, the nature of care in intensive care requires the frequent assessment by X-ray of the patient's chest. Nevertheless, the dangers of repeated exposure to X-rays would not support its routine use several times a day, to check the position of the gastric tube (Adams, 1994). The nurse must therefore use the best method available but with the awareness that no method is 100% accurate and so vigilance must always be encouraged.

Method	Comment
Aspiration of tube	Content is consistent in appearance and consistency with gastric contents.
Auscultation of insufflated air	Listen to stomach with stethoscope for noises that are consistent with air being pushed in.
Check pH of contents aspirated from tube	Contents are assessed for pH. Values of 1.5–5.5 are expected.
Observe for choking or coughing	May not be apparent in the sedated and ventilated patient. Observe tracheal aspirate.
Tube end placed under water — observe for bubbling.	

Feeding regimes

The literature describes two major methods of delivery of enteral feed; continuous or intermittent. However, the terms are interchangeable. Intermittent feeding can describe the method of giving feed as an intermittent bolus or continuously (usually by means of a feeding pump) with regular periods of rest in a twenty-four hour period. Continuous feeding, as it suggests, is the continuous delivery of feed over a twenty-four hour cycle. Links have been established with a rise in the incidence of nosocomial pneumonia and continuous enteral feeding (feeding without rest) due to changes to the pH, rendering it more alkaline. This, it has been proposed, enables bacteria to colonise the stomach and oropharynx which translocate to the respiratory tract causing pneumonia (Jacobs *et al,* 1990; Horwood, 1992; Perry, 1993). A retrospective study of ventilated patients by Lee *et al* (1990) suggests that feeding without rest prevents pH from reaching a bactericidal level which reduces the incidence of colonisation of bacteria. Lee *et al* (1990) report a highly significant reduction in the incidence of pneumonia (from 54% to 12%) in the group of patients who were fed intermittently, in this incidence; fed for 16 hours and fasted for an eight hour period.

It has also been observed that patients who were not receiving any form of enteral feed had an increased risk of septicaemia. This, as mentioned earlier, is thought now to be due to the ischaemic changes as a result of poor blood supply to the gut during periods of severe stress or injury and can contribute to the breakdown of the epithelial cells and tight junctions of the gut wall. Starvation can also cause gut mucosal atrophy as the metabolic demands for a variety of nutrients such as glutamine, are not being provided. The presence of food in the gut also promotes the supply of blood and hormones. Breakdown of the barrier enables bacteria and toxins indigenous to the bowel to translocate into the blood stream (Wilmore *et al*, 1988; Raper and Maynard, 1992; Keithley and Eisenberg, 1993; Spapen *et al*, 1995). Therefore, while bowel rest may be important to maintain an acidic pH, early feeding must also be seen as a priority to maintain gut integrity. But, feeding the patient in intensive care unit via the enteral route is not without its problems. Abdominal distension and cramps, regurgitation, vomiting, diarrhoea and high residual volumes are regular problems that can result in the discontinuation of feed which contributes to the patient's malnourished state. These observations have led researchers into determining the most effective feeding regime, ie. one that does not associate itself with a rise in nosocomial pneumonia, abdominal distension, vomiting or diarrhoea and one that maintains the integrity of the gut wall and immunocompetence (Metheny, 1996). Kacan and Hickish (1986) studied 34 patients in a neurologic intensive care in order to discover whether intermittent or continuous feeding would reduce the incidence of loose stools and aspiration as these were problems felt to be of a high incidence in the neurologically compromised patient in intensive care. Kacan and Hickish (1986) found that the incidence of loose stools/diarrhoea was unchanged in both groups and that both groups reached their calorific requirements at the same time. They also reveal that the incidence of high gastric residual volumes which can cause abdominal distension leading to regurgitation of feed, vomiting and aspiration, were not significantly different between groups. Slow gut motility due to illness and certain drugs can contribute to high residual volumes (Heyland *et al*, 1995). This can be overcome when using the small bowel feeding route and drugs such as metoclopromide for nausea and cisapride or erythromycin to improve gut motility. A study by Williams (1996) however, did not find any significant benefits in their administration.

Monitoring complications and patients safety

While the enteral route is preferred in that it may reduce the incidence of sepsis caused by bacteria colonising invasive feeding lines or the breakdown of the gut wall, it is not without it's own complications:

- feeding tube related — inadvertent placement in the respiratory tract causing aspiration or perforation or oesophageal or nasopharyngeal perforation
- feeding regime related — nosocomial pneumonia attributed to continuous feeding regimes or nausea, abdominal pain cramps, high residual volumes, associated with poor tolerance of the feed or its rate of administration

- biochemical disturbance — hyperglycaemia, hypo-kaleamia, hyperphosphotaemia, vitamin deficiencies and liver function enzyme disturbance
- diarrhoea.

Diarrhoea is a problem that may have serious consequences for sick patients who may already be malnourished. Adam (1994) suggests that the incidence of diarrhoea whether caused by feed or other factors is between 20–40% in the critically ill.

Diarrhoea may cause further electrolyte imbalance, infection as a result of skin breakdown, and is costly in terms of time and patient outcome as well as causing distress to both the patient and the nurse. The development of diarrhoea is often cited in practice as the reason for discontinuation of feed, blame attached to the feed itself. This will therefore contribute further to the malnourished state of the patient. Diarrhoea though may be caused by a number of factors. The overgrowth of bacteria in bowel as a result of antibiotic therapy (Guenter *et al*, 1991 cited by Adam, 1994) and high osmolar drugs, gastric dysfunction due to the cause or severity of illness have all been implicated as causes of diarrhoea. Feed is an excellent medium for bacteria to grow. Contamination of the feed may occur during its preparation or during manipulation of the administration set. Bacteria can then multiply while the feed is hanging at the patients bedside (Farley, 1988). Bacterial contamination of feed has also been implicated as a cause of diarrhoea. Mikschl *et al* (1990) studied the incidence of diarrhoea in relation to the manipulation of the feeding lines causing contamination as well as the techniques used to mix feed and the length of time it is left hanging. Sterile, ready prepared feeds that are connected to sterile administration sets which are changed every 24 hours have been shown to be rarely contaminated (Mikschl *et al*, 1990). Whereas those feeds that require mixing and additions have a higher incidence of contamination. Interestingly though, Mikschel *et al* also found that contamination of the feed was not a significant factor for the development of diarrhoea. Indeed, the incidence of diarrhoea appeared to correlate with the nutritional status of the patient which was a finding reported by earlier researchers. Furthermore, in a study of critically ill patients Levinson and Bryce (1993), found no relationship between the incidence of diarrhoea and feed in ICU.

This implies that in order to reduce the incidence of diarrhoea, factors such as contamination and type of feed should not be immediately considered as the culprit with a subsequent withdrawal of feed. Causes such as the severity of illness and subsequent gastro-dysfunction should be corrected.

There are many aspects of care relating to the provision of enteral nutrition that are beyond the scope of this chapter. There is a burgeoning interest in the use of amino acids such as glutamine and arginine in enteral and parental feeds. These substances and others are being used to maintain cell proliferation in the gut to prevent gut wall breakdown.

Knowledge and education on the provision of nutrition in the critically ill has also been identified as an area in much need of development. An inconsistent approach to providing nutrition could result in the patient being deprived of calories, prolonging healing and lengthening ICU and hospital stay. Some centres have developed nutrition teams which include intensive care nurses to assist in assessing and monitoring nutrition. Arguably, the intensive care nurse is best placed to form the first assessment of nutritional status and has a responsibility to ensure that a nutritional programme is implemented and that alimentary progress is regularly evaluated. In view of the complications that can occur if this care is denied or inadequate, assessment, planning and monitoring of nutritional status should be considered as a nursing priority of care.

References

Adam SK (1994) Aspects of current research in enteral nutrition in the critically ill. *Care of the Crit Ill* **10**(6)

Bastow MD (1988) Complications of enteral feeding. *Gut* **27**(1): 4–6

Berger R, Adams L (1989) Nutritional support in the critical care setting (Part 1). *Chest* July 1

Briggs D (1996a) What type of nasogastric tube should we use in the intensive care unit? *Intensive Crit Care Nurs* **12**: 102–5

Briggs D (1996b) Nasogastric feeding practice in intensive care units: a study. *Nurs Standard* **10**(49): 42–45

Endacott R (1993) Nutritional support for critically ill patients. *Nurs Standard* **7**(52): 25–28

Farley J (1988) Current trends in enteral feeding. *Crit Care Nurse* **8**(4): 23–28

Field J (1988) Enteral tubes at home. *Dist Nurs* **2**(1): 4–6

Goodinson MS (1986) Assessment of nutritional status. *Nursing* **7**: 252–257

Heyland D, Cook DJ, Winder B *et al* (1995) Enteral nutrition in the critically ill patient. A prospective survey. *Crit Care Med* **23**(6): 1055–1060

Holmes S (1987) Nutrition in the critically ill. *Nursing* **15**: 561–566

Horwood A (1990) Malnourishment in intensive care units, as high as 50%: are nurses doing enough to change this? *Intensive Care Nurs* **6**: 205–208

Horwood A (1992) A literature review of recent advances in enteral feeding and the increased understanding of the gut. *Intensive Crit Care Nurs* **8**: 185–188

Jacobs S, Chang RWS, Lee B *et al* (1990) Continuous enteral feeding: a major cause of pneumonia among ventilated intensive care unit patients. *J Parental Enteral Nutrition* **14**(4): 353–356

Jones BM (1986) Enteral feeding: techniques of administration. *Gut* **27**: 47–50

Kacan M, Hickish S (1986) A comparison of continuous and intermittent enteral nutrition in NICU patients. *J Neurosci Nurs* **18**: 333–337

Keithley JK, Eisenberg P (1993) The significance of enteral nutrition in the intensive care patient. *Crit Care Nurs Clinics N Am* **5**(1): 23–29

Lee B, Chang RWS, Jacobs S (1990) Intermittent nasogastric feeding: a simple and effective method to reduce pneumonia among ventilated ICU patients. *Clin Intensive Care* **1**(3)

Levinson M, Bryce A (1993) Enteral feeding, gastric colonisation and diarrhoea in the critically ill patient : is there a relationship? *Anaesth Intensive Care* **21**: 85–8

McWhirter J, Pennington CR (1994) Incidence and recognition of malnutrition in hospital. *Br Med J* **308**(6934): 945–948

Metheny N (1993) Minimizing respiratory complications of nasoenteric tube feedings: state of the science. *Heart Lung* **22**(3): 213–223

Metheny N, Dettenmeier P, Hampton K *et al* (1990) Detection of inadvertent respiratory placement of small-bore feeding tubes. *Heart Lung* **19**: 631-8

Metheny N, Williams P, Wiersema L *et al* (1989) Effectiveness of pH measurements in predicting feeding tube placement. *Nurs Research* **38**: 280–5

Metheny N, McSweeney M, Wehrle M *et al* (1990) Effectiveness of the auscultatory method in predicting feeding tube location. *Nurs Res* **39**: 262–267

Metheny N (1996) *Fluid and Electrolyte Nursing Considerations*, 3rd edition. Lippincott, Philadelphia PA

Mikschl DB, Davidson LJ, Flourney DJ *et al* (1990) Contamination of enteral feedings and diarrhoea in intensive care units. *Heart Lung* **19**: 362–370

Neill KM, Rice KT, Ahern HL (1993) Comparison of two methods of measuring gastric pH. *Heart Lung* **22**(4)

Norton B (1996) Nutritional assessment. *Nurs Times* **92**(26)

Perry L (1993) Gut feelings about gut feeding: enteral feeding for ventilated patients in a district general hospital. *Intensive Crit Care Nurs* **9**: 171–176

Raper S, Maynard N (1992) Feeding the critically ill patient. *Br J Nurs* **1**(6): 273–280

Reilly JJ, Hull SF, Albert N (1987) Economic impact of malnutrition: a model system for hospitalised patients. *J Parental Enteral Nutrition* **12**: 372–376

Scanlon F, Dunne J, Toyne K (1994) No more cause for neglect introducing a nutritional assessment tool and action plan. *Prof Nurse* March: 382–385

Shaw JE (1994) A worrying gap in nurses' knowledge of enteral feeding practice. *Prof Nurse* July

Silk DBA (1994) *Organisation of Nutritional Support in Hospitals*. BAPEN, London

Spapen J, DuinslaegerL, Diltoer M *et al* (1995) Gastric emptying in critically ill ICU patients is accelerated by adding cisapride to a standard feeding protocol. *Crit Care Med* **23**: 481–485

Taylor S, Goodinson-McLaren S (1992) *Nutritional Support: A Team Approach*. Wolfe Publishing, London

Verity S (1996) Nutrition and its importance to intensive care patients. *Intensive Crit Care Nurs* **12**: 71–78

Williams A (1996) The effects of Cisapride on gastric stasis intensive care patients. *Br J Intensive Care* **6**(6): 186–193

Wilmore DW, Smith RJ, O'Dwyer ST *et al* (1986) The gut: a central organ after surgical stress. *Surgery* **104**: 917–923

Zainal G (1994) Nutrition of critically ill people. *Intensive Crit Care Nurs* **10**:165–170

6

Managing the nursing priorities in the patient with an acute myocardial infarction

The aim of this chapter is to discuss the contemporary priorities of care for patients who have suffered from an acute myocardial infarction (AMI).

Objectives of this chapter are:

- to describe the causes and pathogenesis of coronary heart disease and their relationship to cardiac syndromes
- to examine and discuss the assessment priorities for nursing care in patients suffering with an AMI
- to discuss current management and nursing interventions for this group of patients which may assist them to regain control and to adopt a healthy life style once discharged
- to outline in brief the complication of MI.

The majority of patients with acute MI are admitted to coronary care units (CCU), although many intensive care units accept all critically ill persons and some may have patients transferred to them due to bed shortages in the former.

At present, coronary heart disease (CHD) accounts for more than a quarter of all deaths in England in 1992 (DOH, 1994) with an 84% mortality affecting those over 65 years. Geographically, Northern England, Scotland and Northern Ireland have the highest rates of heart disease and mortality. The statistics also indicate that approximately 170, 000 deaths can be attributed to CHD, with one in three men and one in four women dying as a result of this disease (DOH, 1994). Thompson (1996) suggests that the burden of CHD translates to around 30% of all acute medical beds being occupied by patients with this condition. Indeed, treating these patients adds to around 4% of National

Health Service expenditure (DOH, 1994) and the loss of work days places heavy financial loses to British industry in terms of production. However, there is evidence that the trends in mortality and morbidity are declining, probably as a result of improvements in primary and secondary prevention and in treatment (Hunink *et al*, 1997; McGovern *et al*, 1996).

Causes of coronary artery disease and identification of patient problems

The term CHD, refers to the effects of a restricted or lack of blood supply to myocardial tissue which may present in a patient as angina, heart failure, myocardial infarction, dysrhythmias and sudden death. CHD is also synonymous with coronary artery disease (CAD) and ischaemic heart disease (IHD), however all three describe a process where there is diminished blood supply to the heart muscle, leading to either myocardial ischaemia or necrosis, or both (Davies, 1989). These changes do not begin until middle age but may be exacerbated through various lifestyle behaviours and familial factors.

Risk factors

The risk factors associated with CHD are well established, and the presence of more than one or a combination of risk factors increases the potential for morbidity and mortality. Of those listed below, the first three are predictive of CHD but are also modifiable, although at least half of all who are diagnosed with the disease are free from these recognised risk factors:

- smoking
- hypertension
- hyperlipidaemia (raised total cholesterol, and a low ratio to HDL cholesterol)
- lack of physical activity (Wannamethee *et al*, 1995)
- obesity
- diabetes Millitus
- age and gender (immodifiable)

- genetic predisposition/family history (immodifiable).

Regardless of these factors, the prevalence of CHD increases with advancing age, with men aged 55 to 64 years most at risk. However women will experience comparable rates of mortality but these will occur a decade after those in men (Lindsay and Gaw, 1997). This difference is due to the beneficial effects of oestrogen in pre-menopausal women which provides protection from CHD. It is equally suggested that women will suffer more severe infarcts because their disease will be more advanced and because women tend to have smaller coronary vessels when compared to men, thus the incidence of occlusion is high (Jensen and King, 1997). Moreover, women with MI delay in seeking medical advice and being more elderly, they are more likely to be excluded from aggressive treatment (Clark *et al*, 1994; Hannaford *et al*, 1994).

Development and progression of atherosclerosis

Changes affecting the delivery of blood flow within coronary arteries are associated with the development and progression of atherosclerosis. Evidence from coronary angiography and post-mortems demonstrate, that there is a relationship between AMI and atherosclerotic plaque formation, with lesions developing at varying rates and coronary thrombi being able to lyse spontaneously (De Bono, 1994; Forrester, 1991; Fuster *et al*, 1992). Moreover, it is equally possible for plaques to evolve in unaffected segments of coronary vessels while nearby stenotic regions remain unchanged. However, plaques usually form where there is turbulent blood flow and where vessels bifurcate.

Atherosclerotic plaques are described as complex arrangements composed of a lipid pool, smooth muscle cells, macrophages, T lympocytes, collagen and connective tissue which affect the intimal layer of medium and large arterial vessels. The process of atherogenesis begins with the binding of macrophages, T lympocytes and platelets to the endothelial wall of a coronary artery. Under the influence of growth factors, these smooth muscle cells are stimulated to migrate between cells of the sub-endothelium where they begin to proliferate forming fibrous tissue or a fibrointimal lesion (Forrester, 1991;Teplitz and Siwik, 1994). In addition, due to this structural disruption, the shape and thickness of the endothelial membrane will alter.

At present, plaques are classified into fatty streaks, fibrous and advanced complex lesions (Teplitz and Siwik, 1994) but this discussion will concentrate on the two most significant. A **fibrous plaque** develops after the third decade of life and projects outwards into the lumen of the artery. Fibrous lesions are caused by the accumulation and growth of layers of smooth muscle cells which develop into a dense fibrous or collagen cap within the intimal layer of an artery. In time, a fibrous dome migrates onto the surface where it is exposed (*Figure 6.1*). Within the core, is a lipid pool which comprises tiers of cholesterol crystals and cell debris. Fibrous plaques can extend by damaging and exposing the endothelial border or protrude outwards and reduce the circumference of the affected artery (Davies, 1997; Teplitz and Siwik, 1994).

This is unlike **advanced complex lesions** which occur either by platelets adhering rigidly to the fibrous cap forming a thrombus or by the rupture of a plaque. According to Forrester (1991), the formation of a platelet-rich clot on the surface of an existing plaque can abruptly produce partial narrowing of the vessel lumen (*Figure 6.2a*), although if the thrombus is large enough total occlusion of the affected artery is likely (*Figure 6.3a*). It is also possible for fragments of the thrombus to become detached and embolise at a small distal branch resulting in a micro-infarction, haemodynamic dysfunction, and regional hypokenesis (Forrester, 1991) or even sudden death (Weston, 1993).

In the instance of deep plaque fracture, the exposure of the lipid core with blood components will stimulate platelet adhesion which in turn precipitates the formation of an intraluminal thrombus (*Figure 6.2b*). The most frequent site for fissuring is at the junction of the lesion with the normal intima and the plaques most likely to rupture contain a lipid rich core, >40% volume (Davies, 1997). However, plaque morphology and macrophage content have a bearing on whether fissuring occurs (Fuster *et al*, 1992). With regards to plaque rupture this is often unpredictable and may be caused by mechanical stresses due to patterns of blood flow, or toxins (nicotine), coronary artery spasm and other localised factors within the vessel wall (Burke *et al*, 1997; Fuster *et al*, 1992).

Figure 6.1: Evolution of fibrous plaque formation

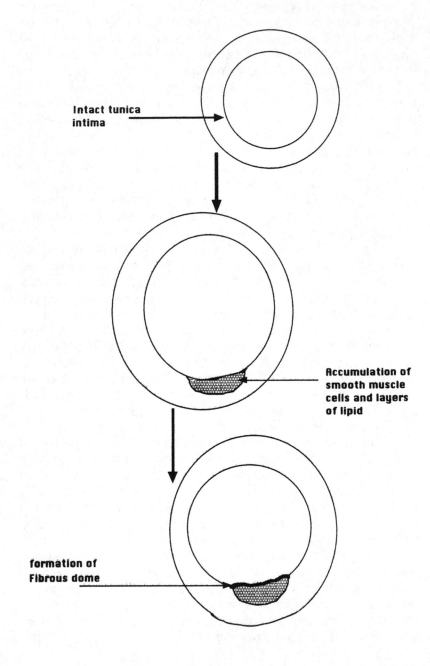

Intact tunica
intima

Accumulation of
smooth muscle
cells and layers
of lipid

formation of
Fibrous dome

With a plaque tear there are a number of possibilities open. The thrombus may completely block the vessel (*Figure 6.2c*) resulting in an AMI or sudden death. A small portion of the clot may also come away and lodge in a capillary downstream with abrupt consequences for the patient. The thrombus may however remain attached on the site of the fractured surface extending its dimensions and occupying a larger luminal section, thus reducing the size of the arterial radius (*Figure 6.3a*). A patient may present with progressive unstable angina. Hence as the fissure heals, the thrombus becomes reconfigured as a new expanded plaque and worsens the degree of stenosis (*Figure 6.3b*). Physical exercise in a situation such as this, will accentuate myocardial oxygen demand and the patient may complain of anginal symptoms. In essence, it would appear that a thrombotic incident is never a static process in so far that it creates a spectrum of options within the affected artery, of which spontaneous lysis is another possibility (Fuster *et al*, 1992; Rozenman and Gotsman, 1994). Moreover, it seems that plaque rupture is a more common cause of luminal thrombosis than the adherence of platelets to an exposed site of a coronary vessel (Davies, 1997).

The implications of platelet aggregation and plaque tear are far reaching. This is because of the simultaneous release of local vasoactive agents (thromboxane, serotonin), resulting in luminal constriction, endothelial membrane erosion (due to the activation of oxygen free radicals), and the proliferation and accumulation of smooth muscle cells (Teplitz and Siwik, 1994). The effects of vasospasm will intensify the severity of regional ischaemia particularly if this occurs proximal to the main stem of the coronary arteries. However, the direct effects of vessel constriction on a pre-existing stenotic area are profound. It is accepted that damage to the endothelial surface, platelet aggregation as well as their activation and thrombi formation are all responsible for a range of cardiac syndromes and the progression of atheromatous plaques (De Bono, 1994; Forrester, 1991).

The evolution of plaques has other adverse effects, namely loss of endothelial membrane properties which are essential for regulating vascular tone (Futterman and Lemberg, 1997). In health, endothelial derivative relaxing

Figure 6.2: Formation and consequences of intra-coronary thrombus

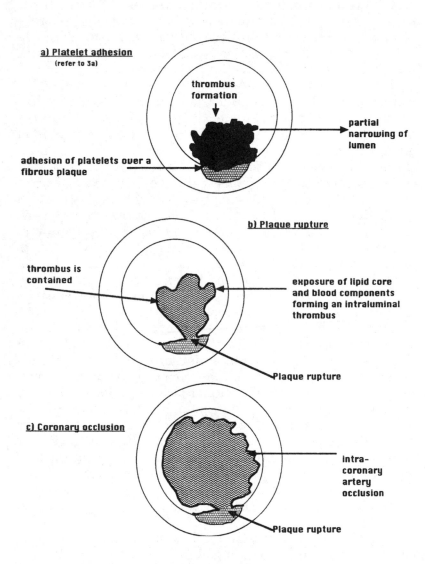

a) **Platelet adhesion**
(refer to 3a)

thrombus formation

partial narrowing of lumen

adhesion of platelets over a fibrous plaque

b) **Plaque rupture**

thrombus is contained

exposure of lipid core and blood components forming an intraluminal thrombus

Plaque rupture

c) **Coronary occlusion**

intra-coronary artery occlusion

Plaque rupture

Figure 6.3a: Possible consequences of platelet aggregation

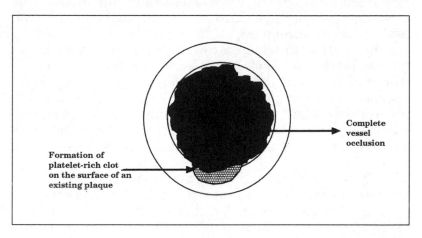

Figure 6.3b: Possible consequences of plaque rupture

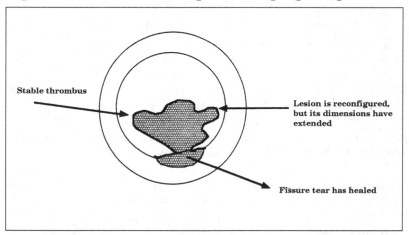

factor (EDRF, an endogenous nitric oxide, NO) is continuously released from the intact lining of the endothelium by the movement of blood, which in turn activates the secretion of nitric oxide and prostacyclin (PGI_2) in order to promote vessel dilatation/relaxation, prevent platelet adhesion and inhibit smooth muscle cell growth. However, these protective mechanisms and functions cease to be available when the endothelial surface is disrupted, particularly in susceptible areas, such as where there is vessel curvature, shear stress and turbulent blood flow.

These changes will produce a local unstable environment that is prone to extremes of vasospasm and vulnerable to the formation of thrombi. Further, since the dilatory wall reserve is compromised, the vessel is also unable to accommodate sudden increases in maximal blood flow across regions of severe stenosis and so worsens the prognostic outcome. However, the use of nitrates reproduces parallel responses of vessel dilation and platelet inhibition through the corresponding activation of cyclic GMP (guanosine monophosphate, a second messenger) and so their role in the management of coronary syndromes is crucial (Wilhelmsen, 1994).

It is nevertheless likely for morphologically complex plaques to develop in patients in the absence of symptoms particularly where the disease has been chronic (Braunwald, 1996; Chester *et al*, 1996). It is also speculated that in older patients with advanced vessel disease, the collateral circulation may be well established and 'conditioned,' thus only smaller myocardial infarctions are experienced (Braunwald, 1996) and this may also account for 'silent ischaemia'. This is unlike 15% of younger patients, who die without warning but have evidence of single vessel disease at autopsy (Weston, 1993). Similarly, in a comparative study, Airaksinen *et al* (1995) reported that ventricular ectopics and chest pain during coronary angioplasty were more evident in patients with less advanced disease, and this was attributed to an underdeveloped auxiliary vasculature. The role of collateral circulation in determining the clinical course can be viewed as relevant in explaining the degree of ischaemic changes experienced by patients.

Stewart (1992) summarises by suggesting that the interplay between intimal injury, dynamic artery wall changes, endothelial wall dysfunction, platelet adhesion and underlying coronary atherosclerosis are all active in the development and progression of CAD. The outcome of this interaction is also dependent on a number of factors which include, severity of oxygen demand, duration of ischaemic episode, oxygen requirements at the time and the amount of collateral blood supply to the affected region.

Patients presenting with AMI do not always arrive at hospital departments immediately following onset of symptoms, often they delay reporting their chest pain. A variety of factors seem to influence the decision not to seek treatment early. Reilly *et al*, (1994) reported that predictors of delayed referral to hospital were dependent on whether the individual perceived the symptoms as serious and of cardiac origin, and whether the onset of pain was witnessed by a family member or friend. Another study reports that when patients' symptoms of heart disease are in congruence with their expectations this influences a person's behaviour to seek treatment sooner (Johnson and King, 1995). It also appears that women and those of advancing age delay in reporting when compared to men and younger patients (Rowe, 1996). Dempsey *et al*, (1995) for example, discovered that women fail to acknowledge the severity of their symptoms until they have exhausted their coping mechanisms or strategies in an effort to minimise threat and to regain control over the event, elements which accounted for their delay in presentation with chest pain. Rowe (1996) also explains that the timing of the event and ethnic background are variables which may motivate individuals to act and seek help. The implications of these studies are that among the primary interventions to be employed by nursing staff should be the education of patients, family and friends in symptom recognition and the importance of not delaying hospital admission. In this country problems between hold-up and treatment have been encountered when patients contact their general practitioner first rather than the emergency services, as well as during transit to and within the hospital (Birkenhead 1992). Such issues raise concern about the means of overcoming the delay in seeking treatment in order for patients to benefit from the early administration of thrombolysis (Boersma *et al*. 1996; Clark *et al*, 1994).

Assessing the priorities for nursing care

The patient with an AMI (transmural, or partial thickness) will describe a range of symptoms, including prolonged intense central chest pain which may radiate to both arms, neck or jaw, and which may be associated with rhythm disturbances (Fowler, 1981). Though, in a quarter of patients with AMI there are no symptoms (Hicks, 1994; Rozenman and Gotsman, 1994). In addition, the patient may be breathless, clammy, sweaty, feel nauseous and distressed.

Patients with AMI will have experienced their pain for a prolonged period usually longer than half an hour, unlike those with a sudden episode of angina whose discomfort may be rapidly alleviated with GTN spray or sublingual tablets, oxygen and rest.

In the acute situation, rapid analysis of symptoms is necessary for the diagnosis and management of ischaemic pain as well as for preventing the sequelae of physiological responses, including dysrhythmias, coronary artery vasospasm, increase in myocardial infarct size and sudden death. Conducting an accurate assessment will also provide a clinical profile of those most at risk of complications of MI (Golman *et al*, 1996) distinguishing patients with differential chest pain (Kernicki 1993), and ensure that they are referred to an appropriate ward (Rozenman and Gotsman, 1994). Therefore, a patient's assessment can contribute to the effective utilisation of available bed resources.

Albarran and Kapeluch (1994) suggested that nurses are often the first point of contact with patients. As such they are in a unique position to utilise their knowledge and skills to identify those individuals most likely to benefit from thrombolytic therapy and/or implement care according to the individual's needs. As timing is crucial, a nurse's contribution can play a major role in terms of patient survival and in maximising myocardial salvage. Decisions taken at this stage will have long term consequences on the patient, thus systematic assessment and collection of relevant clinical data remains an imperative of those involved.

Obtaining a structured history on the nature of the chest pain, including details on severity, pain intensity, location, radiation, associated symptoms, scoring the response to medication and duration is essential in guiding patient care (Kernicki, 1993). The information will begin to establish whether the patient has had an AMI or assist in the management of acute chest pain. The pain history, together with an assessment profile of risk factors play a vital role, as both should alert the nurse to the possibility of myocardial injury.

Pain assessment and control are central to the management of patients, although differentiating symptoms require knowledge and advanced skills as a variety of clinical presentations may mimic myocardial damage (Fruth, 1991).

For example, the use of recreational cocaine and derivative agents has been noted to produce some of the clinical signs associated with MI and should be considered in patients younger than 30 years of age who do not have any known risk factors (Conglio, 1991; Kozlowski-Cepero, 1995). In contrast, of the characteristic approaches employed to diagnose men with MI these do not always apply to women for a variety of factors and this adds to the complexity of chest pain assessment (Holdright, 1996). Indeed, women may present with chest pain suggestive of an ischaemic event but may have normal vessels at angiography (Sullivan *et al*, 1994).

Kernicki (1993) has suggested that patient data can be gathered systematically and proposed a framework based on the mnemonic PQRST (*Table 6.1*). Although Field (1987) and Lekander *et al*, (1993) advance that the success assessment and diagnosis also depends on the nurse's communication and interpersonal skills.

Table 6.1: Patient data (cited in Kernicki, 1993)

P =	precipitating factors (exercise related)
Q =	quality (crushing, or heaviness)
R =	region/radiation (substernal, left and right arm)
S =	associated symptoms/severity (pain score)
T =	timing of symptoms or factors which precipitated pain (nausea, vomiting, dyspnoea)

The assessment of chest pain must be complimented by a measurement of pain severity and even though the available tools are only concerned with intensity. According to Pedley (1996), they provide a measure as to the effectiveness of pharmacology or planned interventions in the care of an individual. Regular assessment using pain scales/meters will equally serve to convey to the patient that their pain has been accepted unconditionally.

An electrocardiogram (ECG) is also vital and early interpretation necessary to confirm or exclude a diagnosis of an ischaemic event (Rozenman and Gotsman, 1994). As front-line clinicians, nurses, can rapidly assess the ECG because they have the necessary skills and expertise (Albarran and Kapeluch, 1994; Caunt, 1992). Changes indicative of MI are manifest by the presence of ST segment elevation, the evolution of Q waves, and symmetrical T wave inversion in the leads where the damage has occurred. Similarly, a chest X-ray can aid by eliminating non-cardiac causes of chest pain, such as fractured ribs, pulmonary embolism, and an aortic dissection. The effects of sub-lingual GTN can equally be one means of gauging whether the patient's pain is of cardiac origin.

Serum cardiac enzymes are chemical markers released as a result of myocardial muscle damage. Typically there are two key enzymes that are of significance for determining whether the patient has had an MI, these are Creatinine Kinase (CKMB which is particular to myocardial muscle but is also found in other areas in smaller amounts) and Lactate Dehydrogenase (LDH which is widely distributed in the body). A rise in serum CKMB above baseline will occur 3–8 hours following myocardial damage and peak at 12–24 hours, although a return to baseline levels may take up to 72 hours. In contrast, serum LDH rises later, usually 24–48 hours after cellular trauma and peaks at 72 hours remaining elevated for several days up to a fortnight (Fox, 1995; Owen, 1995). It is thus useful for diagnosing patients who may have suffered an MI but delayed reporting their pain for more than 24 hours and when CKMB may have reverted to baseline levels. The degree of enzyme rise has been used for crudely estimating the severity of the infarction but it is acknowledged that other factors may produce an increase in cardiac enzymes including anginal syndromes, heart failure, cardiac surgery and tachyarrhythmias. More recent investigations have focused on Troponin T, a protein found in mainly myocardial muscle, which is reportedly a more highly sensitive indicator of myocardial cell injury, whose presence in the circulation (as early as 4–6 hours) can permit a prompt and accurate diagnosis of MI and unstable angina (Antman *et al*, 1996; Fox, 1995; Hamm *et al*, 1992). In addition, as it is untraceable in healthy individuals, an absence of Troponin T from a single sample within the first 10–12 hours following an episode of chest pain can reliably discriminate between those without myocardial damage and thus lead to the effective utilisation of available resources

(Banerjee *et al*, 1997). However, monitoring and recording of blood pressure, heart rate and rhythm as well as the nature of symptoms remain equally important as these, observations will guide the nurse to prioritise and implement the appropriate actions that will promote the patients recovery (Albarran and Kapeluch, 1994). The assessment will also serve to reveal those patients in whom thrombolytic therapy would be unsuitable because of the increased risk of bleeding, and enable their referral to a more appropriate setting. Moreover, the information should provide a framework from which to address their educational requirements, as it seems that patient perceptions on the causes of CAD vary considerably (Greenwood *et al*, 1996; Zerwick *et al*, 1997).

With regards to the assessed problems faced by the patient, these can be divided into four broad areas:

- chest pain that has been persistent for a considerable length of time, not relieved by rest or GTN. The patient may also feel nauseous, have vomited or feel short of breath

- anxiety and fear due to being admitted to a strange and alien environment. The break from usual routines, the atmosphere of a unit and impact of technology, can precipitate additional stress on the patient leading to vasoconstriction of coronary arteries. This is mediated through the release of catecholamines which will increase myocardial workload and expand the degree of tissue damage as well as cardiac instability (Ingham, 1988)

- for many patients, their knowledge and awareness of CAD may need expanding, according to their needs and where there are erroneous assumptions these should clarified in an informed manner

- unstable myocardial function, the risk of ventricular dysrhythmias is high, this may include ventricular fibrillation or tachycardia. In addition, this may also jeopardise cardiac output, thus the patient may be peripherally cold and feel clammy.

Management of a patient's care

Table 6.2: Priorities of care for the patient with AMI

Nursing priority	Intervention/managment
Control and relief of chest pain	• annalgesia • pain scoring • oxygen therapy
Preventing myocardial damage and cardiac instability	• maintenace of myocardial reperfusion • monitoring cardiovascular parameters and the effects of cardiac drugs
Promoting optimal physical and emotional recovery	• providing emotional support and promoting independence • family involvement • meeting educational needs
Preparing the patient for discharge from CCU	• planning ward transfer with the patient • maintaining the patient informed
Prevention of complications	• monitoring and recognition of changes

Control and relief of chest pain

In terms of pain control, intravenous diamorphine remains the primary opiate of choice for these patients. The benefit extends beyond pain relief, in that it helps to reduce anxiety and the effects of sympathetic overactivity, thereby decreasing myocardial instability and workload and may limit the size of ischaemic damage (Antman, 1994; Jowett and Thompson, 1995). Typically, doses range between 2.5–10mgs, although Townsend (1988) reported that patients indicated that a bolus of 5mgs was the most effective and Gaston-Johanson *et al*, (1991), suggest that this can be repeated up to a maximum of 20–25mgs within 12 hours. An intravenous route by way of a cannula is preferred, as it achieves rapid pain relief allowing for repeated doses but without influencing enzyme measures due to repeated tissue trauma. The nurse must record the pain score regularly, including respiratory rate and blood pressure as both may fall with additional doses when given over a short period.

Intravenous nitrates are also rapid acting and may be

given in tandem with diamorphine in the acute phase, providing the systolic is greater than 110mmHg. Nitrates reduce venous return (preload) and vascular resistance (afterload) so improving the overall performance of the heart and decreasing oxygen demands. At higher doses nitrates will dilate coronary arteries enhancing tissue perfusion and leading to symptomatic relief of chest pain but this can be accompanied by a noticeable reduction in blood pressure (Willhelmsen, 1994). It is advised that the infusion is judiciously titrated with pain scores and blood pressure recordings in order to avoid a sudden drop in perfusion. Once over the acute phase there are other means of delivering nitrate therapy, including sub-lingually, orally and transdermally.

The titration of drugs as well as regular measurement of pain intensity by way of either a verbal descriptor scale (for example, Berker and Hughes, 1990) visual analogue scale (for example, Thompson *et al*, 1994) or numerical rating scales (for example, Bondestam *et al*, 1987) will assist the practitioner in gauging the effectiveness of treatment, secure an element of objectivity and compliment the qualitative data (Jacavone and Dostal, 1992; Pedley, 1996). This is of importance as it is suggested that as many as 80% of patients leave CCU without reporting their pain or discomfort even though they are aware of the severity of their symptoms (Mackintosh, 1994; Schneider, 1987). This has implications regarding how chest pain is assessed, as without accurate evaluation the individual may be mis-managed, as such, claims of negligence in this area will increase (Small, 1996). It therefore seems prudent that patients should be educated early on about the importance of their symptoms and why their discomfort must be acted upon as soon as it develops. Basilicato *et al*, (1992) in a randomised trial studied the effects of maintaining a chest discomfort diary. Their findings suggest that this strategy taught patients how to report their symptoms and improve the accuracy of their subjective accounts when compared to the control group. This could reasonably be adopted while in hospital and maintained at home as record of changes in their symptoms, and act as a guide in future consultations and in planning therapeutic interventions.

Oxygen therapy should also commence immediately as

it will assist with tissue oxygenation and prevent the extension of myocardial ischaemia, which may develop secondary to a combination of poor left ventricular function and pulmonary congestion caused as a result of AMI (Antman, 1994; Baas, 1996). Nasal prongs or face mask, depending on which is more tolerable should be maintained for between 24 to 48 hours at a rate 2–4 litres/minute (100%), aiming for oxygen saturation of greater than 95%. As patients often complain of a dry mouth, small sips or ice cubes may provide comfort, particularly if fluid is restricted. By contrast, limiting metabolic oxygen requirements can also be achieved by dietary management, namely by ensuring that meals are light, palatable, and containing a balance of kilocalories according to size and gender. Further, reducing the strain of faecal elimination by the administration of an apperient or lactulose can also minimise oxygen consumption and myocardial workload. In more severe cases of poor oxygenation, a period of mechanical ventilation may be required to correct hypoxaemia and support heart function.

Preventing myocardial damage and cardiac instability

Caunt (1992) and Antman (1994) have suggested that in the last three decades coronary care practice has developed rapidly since the introduction of the first specialist units and has now entered the 'reperfusion era,' where the aims are focused on restoring blood flow in the diseased artery and preventing coronary vessel reocclusion. The advent of thrombolysis, (whose function is to activate plasminogen into plasmin and lyse the freshly formed thrombus) has revolutionised the management of patients with a myocardial infarction resulting in reduced complications and mortality rates. The most widely available thrombolytics are streptokinase, alteplase (rt-PA) and anistreplase, the former is most commonly prescribed and the least expensive.

The clinical trials have further demonstrated that the anti-platelet effects of aspirin administered as soon as possible when combined with thrombolytics, reduce hospital mortality from AMI substantially (International Study of Infarct Survival, ISIS-2, 1988). In addition, the evidence suggests that the advantages of this therapy are most likely if the patient receives the drug within 1–6 hours from the onset of chest discomfort (Boersma *et al*, 1996; Gruppo Italiano per lo Studio nell'Infarcto Miocardio, GISSI, 1986; Weaver, 1996), although the benefits may still be accrued up to 24 hours later. A recent analysis has concluded that, despite comparisons over the clinical effectiveness between alteplase and streptokinase in restoring reperfusion, the trials have failed to illustrate a difference in survival rates between these two thrombolytics (Weaver, 1996). However, because many of the thrombolytics have a short half-life there is the potential for abrupt coronary reocclusion, and nurses by virtue of their close contact are in a position to first discern these signs and act accordingly, thus illustrating their impact on patient outcomes.

Once a patient is identified as suitable for thrombolysis (*Table 6.3*) it is the nurse's role to ensure the safety of the patient and to monitor the effects of the therapy. The potential patient problems include hypotension and allergic reactions (commonly with streptokinase), bleeding, reperfusion dysrhythmias, and coronary artery reocclusion. As patients are principally at risk from haemorrhage during and after the infusion, invasive procedures should be limited and damage/trauma to skin must be avoided. Controlling the risks of bleeding also requires that nurses involve patients in the care, and should encourage them to report any manifestation of haemorrhage, such as gingival bleeds or oozing from existing intravenous cannula sites.

Table 6.3: Inclusion citeria for thrombolysis

ST segment elevation: 1mm in II, III and f AVF; or 1mm I and AVL or 2mm in V1 to V6
Onset of chest pain less than 24 hours, (preferably < 6 hours)
Clinical history: onset of pain, location/radiation, known risk factors, pain unrelieved by GTN
Not contraindicated

To maintain patency of the affected vessel following thrombolysis, clotting parameters of 1.5–2 times the normal range have been sought by administering heparin, initially by intravenous (IV) route and then subcutaneously (SC) until the patient is ambulant. However Yusuf *et al*, (1996) reported that when heparin is added to streptokinase the risks of bleeding increase. Moreover, the studies suggest that regardless of IV or SC route there appears to be no clinical advantages for the patient (Meyer and Chesebro, 1994), thus it is recommended that heparin prescription should be discouraged unless it is for those in whom thrombolytics are contraindicated (Yusuf *et al*, 1996).

Preventing further cardiac instability, also involves continued vigilance partly because of the nature of the patient's condition and in part because of the adverse effects of various cardiac drugs *(Table 6.4)*. This should involve monitoring for new chest pain, evidence of ST elevation on the ECG, evaluating cardiac enzyme trends and the presence of dysrhythmias all of which are indicators of coronary reocclusion, estimated to be in the range 15–25%, although aspirin can reduce the incidence to around 10% (Antoniucci *et al*, 1996; Martin and Kennedy, 1994). Evidence of reocclusion will necessitate interventional management either with rescue percutaneous transluminal coronary angioplasty (PTCA) and/or intracoronary stenting, procedures which are viable even during the acute stages of an MI. PTCA, for example, is a widely accepted technique which is employed to dilate, by means of a balloon, a stenosed coronary artery with the purpose of improving blood flow and relieving the symptoms of coronary ischaemia and angina. It is suitable for those in whom thrombolysis is contra-indicated and where it is desirable to restore higher blood rates than the former may be capable of achieving (Brady and Buller, 1996; de Belder and Thomas, 1997; Grines, 1996). In addition, PTCA has been employed for 'rescue' situations, namely when thrombolytic therapy has failed, the use of PTCA however has resulted in significant improvements in blood flow to the infarct related vessel. In contrast, an intracoronary stent is described as an expandable surgical stainless steel or titanium tube which is inserted by means of a guide wire into the stenosed area with the goal of improving distal blood flow by splinting the diseased site. Indications for stenting include when there have been suboptimal results immediately following PTCA, for new lesions for which a coronary stent is the first choice of treatment, restenosis within six months of PTCA and as a bridge to surgery (Brady and Buller, 1996; Rodriguez *et al*,

1996). Further, in the case of stents, there is a significantly reduced rate of complications and improved patient outcomes compared to PTCA (Antoniucci *et al*, 1996; Neumann *et al*, 1996; Rodriguez *et al*, 1996).

With reference to cardiovascular drugs these have side-effects which may worsen cardiac functioning (*Table 6.4*), thus regular assessment of blood pressure, heart rate and rhythm remains a cornerstone of the critical care nurse's role. Continued evaluation of cardiovascular parameters and ECG trace is clearly necessary as many of these drugs can be prescribed in combination, while improving the patient's condition, they add to the complexity of care. Dysrhythmias, either drug induced or as a complication from AMI, require prompt analysis as many are life-threatening in the acute stages. Nurses must be knowledgeable as to the possible clinical changes and must also be able to explain the rationale of these to the patient and family as this information appears a key concern (Chan, 1990; Czar *et al*, 1997).

Promoting optimal physical and emotional recovery

Reducing patient anxiety is regarded as a major area in which clinical nursing staff can contribute. From being in a state of emotional distress and feeling isolated it is possible for patients to become progressively depressed, a phenomenon that is claimed to occur three days post-MI (Cassem and Hackett, 1973), thus delaying the recovery and resumption of daily activities of living. However, recent data supports the view that anxiety is prevalent in MI patients and may persist up to a year after discharge, whereas depressive symptoms are uncommon (Baas, 1996; Crowe *et al*, 1996). Anxiety and stress levels also fluctuate during hospitalisation, being highest on admission and prior to transfer to a general ward (Schwartz and Brenner, 1979; Crowe *et al*, 1996). Anxiety is a typical reaction in patients with AMI and is triggered by the clinical environment, unit personnel, the sudden nature of hospital admission, social isolation and vunerability with regards to possible death. These emotional symptoms can further aggravate cardiac instability through the ongoing stimulation of adrenergic receptor sites, resulting in coronary vasospasm, tachycardia, raised myocardial contractility and vessel occlusion. Other manifestations of anxiety may include restlessness, intense

Table 6.4: Effects of various cardiac drugs used following AMI

Drug	Actions	Clinical conditions	Side effects
Nitrates	Dilate coronary arteries (in high doses) • reduce preload and afterload • reduce workload of heart and oxygen demand	MI, angina Acute left ventricular failure	Hypotension Headaches Reflex tachycardia Tolerance problems
Angiotensin converting enzyme-inhibitors	Inhibit the conversion of angiotensin I, thus reduce preload and afterload • decrease myocardial consumption and ventricular wall tension • inhibit sodium and water reabsorption as aldosterone remains inactivated • diminish potential of left ventricular dilatation	Post AMI and LV dysfunction Congestive heart failure Hypertension	Hypotension Renal impairment Non-productive cough
Calcium channel blockers	Dilate coronary arteries/peripheral vasodilators • decrease myocardial contractility • reduce oxygen consumption Some can alter AV conduction	Hypertension Unstable angina Supraventricular rhythms (verapamil/diltiazem)	Hypotension Flushing Headaches Syncope Bradycardias Negative inotropic effects
Beta-blockers	Block certain receptor sites, reducing heart rate, blood pressure and myocardial contractility • decrease myocardial oxygen demand/workload • minimise the incidence of ventricular disturbances	Post AMI Angina Hypertension	Hypotension Bradycardia Dizzyness/nightmares/depression Contra-indicated in many patients Heart failure

preoccupation with the ECG trace on the monitor, the patient may also be tense, withdrawn or hostile, and unable to concentrate or to communicate adequately.

Many of the behaviours can be attributed to patient's feeling a lack of control or powerlessness to influence any aspect of their situation. Earlier Garrity and Klein (1975) identified that those with ineffective coping mechanisms or who had not adjusted following AMI, were more likely to die within six months after discharge. The implications of the above are that health care staff must influence short and long-term outcomes by identifying health beliefs, returning control to the patient, empowering the individual to the full extent of their abilities, implementing strategies that promote coping and dealing with emotions (Ingham, 1988; Lindquist, 1986). This was achieved in a small trial in which Ziemann and Dracup (1990) introduced a contractual agreement with one group of patients over a range of aspects such as, family visits, daily hygiene routines, health teaching, activity and environment. Their findings demonstrated that those in the experimental group had significantly reduced levels of anxiety and hostility, because the unique approach had enhanced a sense of control and facilitated early emotional adaptation.

Conditional to the success of nurses in supporting those with an AMI is effective nurse-patient communication. Nurses by their intimate and continued proximity with their patients will be viewed as key sources of information. Garrity and Klein (1975) claim that the quality of interactions will also have a direct effect in terms of recovery and early discharge. However, for communication to have meaning, it must be conveyed in terms that are simple and familiar to the recipient, not involving a large number of facts, that is focused on the individual and sufficiently structured to enable understanding. The manner in which practitioners approach the patient is also pertinent. For example, an anxious nurse will communicate certain attitudes to the patient, about expertise, reliance and approachability. Because of the alien nature of the environment, the patient may have a myriad of questions some will be more simple than others, although many may have difficulty in articulating their concerns and being able to perceive that the nurse as a trusted and friendly ally will be reassuring as well as inspire confidence. It is therefore vital, that a firm rapport is established at the earliest opportunity with the patient that will last through the hospital stay. In many instances anticipating some of the general questions that the patient or family may have can begin the process and enable more specific questions to be asked. However, some patients may find it difficult to gain understanding from health care professionals; written materials or audio/video-tapettes can augment or bolster the spoken word.

Thompson (1990) advocates that the close contact between nurse and patient encourages feelings of security in the latter. By prompting patients to discuss their feelings, nurses can assist individuals to identify the sources of stress and redefine their perspective. Indeed, when patients view their MI in negative terms this inhibits an early recovery and resumption of previous work patterns (Petrie *et al*, 1996). By encouraging the patient to focus on attainable short-term goals, presenting an optimistic outlook, highlighting the individual's personal resources and giving them the opportunity to engage in choices over care, can enable the person to become confident about their future and to gain control over their situation (Lindquist, 1986). These strategies can be maximised if there is continued appropriate praise relevant to the activity and if the expectations set are realistic and clearly understood.

Including a family member or the individual who will be involved with the care is paramount. The partner will inevitably feel traumatised by the events, often blaming themselves for the MI and fearing the loss of a mate. These feelings are compounded because they are often excluded from the care of their loved one. Limiting information solely to the patient has other adverse consequences namely in terms of marital friction and conflicts between the couple, particularly once at home. For the spouse or significant carer, the lack of information may lead to over vigilance, as well as being prescriptive and restrictive about their loved one's level of physical activity, actions that are often based on misconceptions and mistaken assumptions about the patient's condition. This has been recently discussed in the context of resuming sexual activity following AMI (Albarran and Bridger, 1997).

One study that involved 46 couples in which men had suffered an AMI, demonstrated that distress in the post infarction period was higher in females when compared to their male partners, and that evidence of depression in the women was linked to the severity of the men's illness and understanding of the disease (Connell and Bennett, 1997). However, the research suggests that spouses benefit from the advice of health experts, although the majority are still not furnished with the approriate level of information to enable them to cope emotionally, to support their partner once discharged home and to understand the effects of an MI (Mongiardi *et al*, 1987; Thompson and Cordle, 1988). On a practical level, any communication affecting the patients' well being should incorporate the partner, as this will serve to clarify the issues and overcome difficulties associated with recall and retention of information experienced in the acute stages (Albarran, 1996).

Connell and Bennett (1997) suggest that social support was one of the factors that helped to protect the couple from emotional distress in the post-MI phase. The role of the family and friends are important for the patient as a source of emotional comfort and social worth, arguably working with them can create a more satisfying and caring experience for those involved. However, Fleury (1993) who questioned 24 patients about the role of social networks in influencing their health behaviour, revealed that these were either enabling or confining. With regards to the latter, social networks could diminish the patient's motivation by challenging his/her health values or expressing an unwillingness to tolerate them, expecting that those with AMI should adhere to pre-determined boundaries of behaviour and activity. Inevitably, as partners participate in joint health education they will develop a stronger awareness of rehabilitation goals and identify a means of supporting their loved one's.

Another way forward is through relaxed visiting policies, as this reduces social isolation and visitors can raise the patients' esteem and self worth. At present, there is little evidence that visits are physiologically detrimental to the majority of patients (Kleman *et al*, 1993) and that current restrictions on visiting seem to have no justification and are based on traditions (Blanchard, 1995). It would appear though, that nurses are increasingly using discretionary judgements rather than adhering to policies with regards to allowing friend and family visits (Simon *et al*, 1997).

Visiting should be balanced with periods of uninterrupted rest and sleep, and negotiating this with the partner is appropriate but any agreement should be adhered to. Alternatively, acknowledging the particular patient preferences and communicating these to any callers, emphasises individualised care. Endeavouring to optimise the quality of sleep and maintaining the normal pattern by planning activities around the patients' needs, as well as minimising noise levels and harsh lighting is also integral to the plan of care. Additionally, if the individual's pain is under control, he/she is fully aware of the unit's routines and his/her personal needs are met, sleep and relaxation are more likely to occur.

Comfort can also be promoted through physical care. Hygiene must be maintained involving the patient according to their ability, and progressing to either shower or bathing when they are more confident. However, in the acute phase they will still need assistance and support. Promoting independence in this area could be through negotiation with the patient, as there may be aspects of care that the individual wishes and is able to assume without physical discomfort. Teaching patients relaxation techniques such as the use of therapeutic massage can reduce anxiety and stress without physiological consequences.

The process of early mobilisation can also create a sense of recovery, strengthen confidence, promote independence and control. Ideally, early ambulation should commence within 24 hours in the uncomplicated MI patient, but this should be graduated according to guidelines but must encompass the patients' clinical status and their physical reserve. Patients who are stable, can be encouraged to mobilise by sitting out of bed the day following admission and progressing to walking around the bed area and lavatories/dining room. According to Jowett and Thompson (1995) this approach reduces the problems associated with bedrest and notions of physical and psychological disability. Moreover, it emphasises to the patient that they are capable of resuming their previous level of physical activity.

Meeting the educational needs of the patient with an

MI must be a primary 'raison d'etre' of the critical care nurse, and it is unequivocal that the imparting of structured and individualised health education is beneficial in promoting physical, social and psychological recuperation as well as rehabilitation (Cay, 1995; Duryée, 1992; Raleigh and Odtohan, 1987; Wang, 1994). One recent national group has developed cardiac rehabilitation guidelines and audit standards in which it is stated that in-hospital education should be specific, coordinated, available in a variety of languages and mediums of communication. The report adds that patient education, '*should start simultaneously with the process of medical diagnosis and management, and its aim is to ensure that patients at all times have accurate and up-to-date understanding...*' (Thompson *et al*, 1996).

Patients not only need to comprehend the complexity of their clinical condition and implications, but also absorb the rationale of various treatments/investigations, be equipped with the knowledge about how to reduce as well as manage their relevant risk factors and be aware of alternative strategies for improving their health. Mirka (1994) indicates that there will be many barriers preventing learning, including pain and discomfort, stress, anxiety and environmental factors. In order to maximise patient learning and secure the retention of information, notice of these features is vital, as is awareness of adult learning theories, and presenting the information in such a way that it is meaningful and reflects the patient's unique needs.

A number of small and large scale studies have illustrated that the patient's and the public's general understanding of the known risk factors, symptoms and the timecourse of the disease is poor, with a number of items such as overwork, stress and worry often being cited as the main causative risk factors (Fielding, 1987; Greenwood *et al*, 1996; Murray 1989; Newens *et al*, 1996; Zerwic *et al*, 1997). Although smoking and being overweight were ranked as physical explanations for an MI and modifiable. On the basis of this, these investigators have argued that education should be targeted to all patients with CAD, in particular those with a known high risk profile such as hypertension and diabetes.

Despite this it would appear that patients are receiving vague and imprecise information on which choices to make, which has concentrated on dietary modification (Murray,

1989). Similarly, in a project involving five trusts, Newens *et al,* (1995) reported that information on areas such as stress and anxiety was very limited, whereas over 68% of men with MI (n=202) had been made familiar with the importance of diet, few had received written details about exercise and less than half had participated in discussions with nurses on this topic. However, respondents to a small study had declared that exercise programmes were one of the most appealing interventions (Campbell *et al*, 1994), presumably from the perceived physical confidence and emotional satisfaction of achievement. It is reasonable to argue that health education of post-MI patients should concentrate on the needs of the patient not on what the health provider perceives as important (Wang, 1994). Otherwise, dissatisfaction of those viewed as key sources will persevere and since the consumers will not identify with the information dessiminated their motivation to learn will remain unstimulated and the spiral of public ignorance remain.

It is evident that patients expect their specific educational priorities to be covered (*Table 6.5*), although the areas required to be addressed seem to alter in rank order as individuals move along a continuum from the critical care setting, to a step-down ward, discharge home and outpatient (OP) clinics. At each of these phases their learning needs appear to differ and as their understanding increases their questioning may become more specific particulalrly when they confront areas of daily living which had not been anticipated as relevant as inpatients, for example resuming sexual activity (Albarran and Bridger, 1997).

It is interesting to note from *Table 6.5*, that patients' perceived learning needs have evolved in a decade, yet some aspects remain consistent. In addition, Czar and Engler (1997) have indicated that there is no correlation between the importance of educational requirements and age, occupation, smoking or marital status. Although from the concerns raised at the first clinic visit after discharge, many of the findings are similar to those described by Cay (1995), namely that at four weeks after first MI patients still wanted information on medications, anatomy and physiology, risk factors, and guidelines on returning to work. This would suggest that health education imparted in CCU needs to be carefully planned, although situations for opportunistic

Table 6.5: Patient's perceptions of areas for cardiac teaching

Author	Sample site	Clinical condition	Priority areas for teaching
Karlik and Yarcheski, 1987	CCU/convalescing at home	MI patients (n=30)	CCU • risk factors • anatomy and physiology • medications • seeking medical advice/ managing symptoms Home • risk factors • medications • anatomy and physiology
Chan, 1990	Step-downward	MI patients (n=30)	• risk factors • anatomy and physiology • medications
Wingate, 1990	CCU/step-downward	MI patients (n=32)	CCU • risk factors • anatomy and physiology • activity Step-downward • anatomy and physiology • risk factors • medications
Czar and Engler, 1997	Step-downward/ OP clinic	Angina and MI patients (n=28)	CCU • symptom recognition • anatomy and physiology • medications OP-clinic • anatomy and physiology • symptom recognition • medications

teaching must also be seized, and delivery must be tailored to the individual's concerns with retention of knowledge as a central objective.

Preparing the patient for discharge from CCU

Discharge from the critical care environment has been identified as significant time for the patient in terms of anxiety, stress and cardiovascular complications. Though transfer from the CCU/ITU may be an indicator of recovery, the patient may have become accustomed to the security, comfort, as well as continued nursing and technological surveillance available in these clinical areas. The patient will have to adjust to new surroundings, the lack of close supervision, ward personnel and gain confidence in those involved in the individuals' care. In addition, family members may interpret the discharge as an opportunity to relax and sort things out at home, and the patient may once again feel separated and left to adjust to the new circumstances.

In the uncomplicated MI, preparation should commence early enabling the individual to begin to become accustomed to resuming self-care, as this may assist with reducing the conceptions of cardiac invalidism. In their small randomised study, Schwartz and Brenner (1979) offered two experimental groups' information about transfer and provided a visit by the admitting ward nurse while patients were in the CCU. The control group received routine care. The findings revealed that the experimental group experienced less cardiovascular complications in the first 24 and 72 hours after transfer as well as lower scores for stress, this also applied to their families. It is concluded that communication and utilising the family as a resource are two ways of enhancing patient care and promoting continuity in the delivery of nursing services.

Other practical aspects include removing the ECG monitoring leads and intravenous cannulae as soon as it is acceptable, providing the patient has remained clinically stable. Stating the planned time for transfer, the name and location of the ward and the telephone extension which will be important to the family. Advising patient and partner about the subsequent timetable of events or investigations, ward routines and visiting policies as well as names of key personnel can facilitate the transition to a new environment (Baas, 1996). The likelihood of expected visitors, such as rehabilitation nurse and dietitian should also be conveyed to the patient to emphasise the process of health education and support. Finally, the patient and family must be reassured that the ward staff will have both a verbal report and continuation notes, the particular stage of recovery and progress with actual problems relevant to them will also be discussed. Finally, Jowett and Thompson (1995) recommend that patients become involved during the handover phase, not only to clarify any issues, but for cementing a relationship between ward staff and the individual.

Preventing complications

With the introduction of thrombolysis the incidence of complications post-MI has decreased, it is presently estimated that the risk of adverse events, (unstable angina, reinfarction, ventricular fibrillation and death) is more likely to occur between days 6–10 after the initial insult (Wilkinson *et al*, 1995). It is further suggested that the risk of a major event declines after the MI, particularly for uncomplicated infarction and heart failure-free individuals. Nevertheless, in the immediate phase, the prospect of a serious complication is high and in the presence of heart failure the prognosis of death is increased. However, Jowett and Thompson (1995) comment that size of MI, loss of functional myocardium and extent of CAD are key determinants as to the severity of the complications. In the vulnerable stages, the continuous monitoring and evaluation of all cardiovascular and psychological parameters are ongoing nursing imperatives. As the range of complications are varied and unpredictable (*Table 6.6*), this requires a nurse's clinical expertise and judgement to be able to rapidly discriminate, anticipate and execute measures that will have an impact on patient outcome.

Table 6.6: Complications following acute MI

• Dysrhythmias (ventricular ectopics, and conduction blocks, cardiac arrest)
• Cardiogenic shock (inadequate myocardial contactility, due to right or left sided failure)
• Heart failure (secondary to pump failure/damage and raised afterload)
• Embolic events, (typically pulmonary embolism/deep vein thrombosis)

- ◆ Left ventricular thrombus (clot from injured wall, dislodges and results in cerebral embolism)

- ◆ Pericarditis (inflammation of pericardium occurring within days post-MI)

- ◆ Cardiac rupture/tamponade (this may be damage to the free wall or septum, prognosis is poor unless there is access for open heart surgery). Papillary muscle damage can also occur but manifest as left ventricular failure and mitral regurgitation.

References

Airakisnen K *et al* (1995) Stenosis severity and the occurrence of ventricular ectopic activity during acute coronary occlusion during balloon angioplasty. *Am J Cardiol* **76**: 346–349

Albarran JW, Kapeluch H (1994) Role of the nurse in thrombolytic therapy. *Br J Nurs* **3**(3): 104–109

Albarran JW (1996) Exploring the nature of informed consent in coronary care practice. *Nurs Crit Care* **1**(3): 127–133

Albarran JW, Bridger S (1997) Problems with providing education on resuming sexual activity after myocardial infarction: developing written information for patients. *Intensive Crit Care Nurs* **13**(1): 2–11

Antman E (1994), General hospital management. In: Julian D, Braunwald E (eds) *Management of acute myocardial infarction*. W B Saunders Company, London

Antman E, Tanasijevic M, Thompson B *et al* (1996) Cardiac-specific troponin I levels to predict the risk of mortality in patients with acute coronary syndromes. *New England J Med* **335**(18):1342–1349

Antoniucci D, Valenti R, Buonamici P *et al* (1996) Direct angioplasty and stenting of the infarct-related artery in acute myocardial infarction. *Am J Cardiol* **78**: 568–571

Baas L (1996) Care of the cardiac patient. In: Kinney M, Packa D (eds) *Andreoli's Comprehensive Cardiac Care*. 8th edition. Mosby, St. Louis: Chap 8

Banerjee S, Straffen A, Rhoden WE (1997) Value of qualitative Troponin T estimation in decision-making in patients with chest pain. *Br J Cardiol* **4**(10): 414–418

Basilicato S, Groves M, Nisbet L *et al* (1992) Effect of concurrent chest pain assessment on retrospective reports by cardiac patients. *J Cardiovasc Nurs* **7**(1): 56–67

Berker M, Hughes B (1990) Using a tool for pain assessment. *Nurs Times* **86**(24): 50–52

Birkenhead JS (1992) Time delays in provision of thrombolytic treatment in six district hospitals. *Br Med J* **205**: 445–448

Blanchard H (1995) Is restricted visiting in conflict with patients' needs. *Br J Nurs* 4(19): 1160–1162

Boersma E, Maas AC, Deckers JW et al (1996) Early thrombolytic treatment in acute myocardial infarction:reappraisal of the golden hour. *The Lancet* 348: 771–775

BodestamE, Hovgren K, Gaston Johansson F *et al* (1987) Pain assessment by patients and nurses in the early phase of acute myocardial infarction. *J Adv Nurs* 12: 677–682

Braunwald E (1996) Acute myocardial infarction — the value of being prepared. *N Engl J Med* 334(1): 51–52

Burke A, Farb A, Malcom G *et al* (1997) Coronary risk factors and plaque morphology in men with coronary disease who died suddenly. *New England J Med* 336(18): 1276–1282

Campbell N, Grimshaw J, Rawles J *et al* (1994) Cardiac rehabilitation: the agenda set by post-myocardial infarction patients. *Health Educ Counselling* 53: 409–420

Cassem NH, Hackett MD (1973) Psychological rehabilitation of myocardial infarction patients in the acute phase. *Heart Lung* 2(3): 382–388

Caunt J (1992) The changing role of coronary nurses. *Intensive Crit Care Nurs* 8(2): 82–93

Cay E (1995) Goals of rehabilitation. In: Jones D, West R (eds) *Cardiac Rehabilitation*. BMJ publishing, London: ch 2

Chan V (1990) Content areas for cardiac teaching: patients' perceptions of the importance of teaching content after a myocardial infarction. *J Adv Nurs* 15: 1139–1145

Chester M, Chen L, Kaski JC (1996) The natural history of unheralded complex coronary plaques. *J Am Coll Cardiol* 28(3): 604–608

Clark K, Gray D, Hampton J (1994) Do women with acute myocardial infarction receive the same treatment as men. *Br Med J* 309: 563–566

Coniglio K (1991) Cocaine-induced acute myocardial infarction. *Crit Care Nurse* 11(2): 16–25

Connell H, Benett P (1997) Anticipating levels of anxiety and depression in couples where the husband has survived a myocardial infarction. *Coron Health Care* 1(1): 22–26

Crowe JM, Runions J, Ebbsen L *et al* (1996) Anxiety and depression after acute myocardial infarction. *Heart Lung* 25(2): 98–107

Czar M, Engler M (1997) Perceived learning needs of patients with coronary artery disease using a questionnaire assessment tool. *Heart Lung* 26(2): 109–117

Davies M (1989) The pathological basis of ischaemic heart disease. *Med Int* 16: 2813–2817.

Davies M (1997) The composition of coronary artery plaques. *New England J Med* 336(18): 1312–1314

De Belder A, Thomas MR (1996) Primary angioplasty for the treatment of actue myocardial infarction. *Br J Hosp Med* 58(1): 35–38

De Bono D (1994) Pathophysiology of ischaemic heart disease. In: De Bono D, Hopkins A (eds) *Management of stable angina*. Royal College of Physcians, London

Brady A, Buller N (1996) Coronary angioplasty and myocardial ischaemia. *Care Crit Ill* **12**(3): 83–86

Dempsey SJ, Dracup K, Moser DK (1995) Women's decision to seek care for symptoms of acute myocardial infarction. *Heart Lung* **24**(6): 444–456

Department of Health (1994) *Coronary heart disease: An epidimological overview*. HMSO, London

Duryée R (1992) The efficancy of in patient education after myocardial infarction. *Heart Lung* **21**(3): 217–227

Dracup K (1995) *Meltzer's intensive coronary care: a manual for nurses*. 5th edition. Prentice Hall International, Conneticut

Field ML (1987) Teaching and interviewing: A three function model. *Dimen Crit Care Nur* **6**(5): 304–312

Fielding R (1987) Patient's beliefs regarding the causes of myocardial infarction: implications for information giving and compliance. *Patient Education Counselling* **9**: 121–134

Fleury J (1993) An exploration of the role of social networks in cardiovascular risk reduction. *Heart Lung* **22**(2): 134–144

Forrester J (1991) Intimal disruption and coronary thrombosis: its role in the pathogenesis of human coronary disease. *Am J Cardiol* **68**: 69b–77b

Fowler N (1981) Diagnosis: Guide to interpretation of chest pain. *Hosp Med* **17**: 12–31

Fox K (1995) Cardiac enzymes. *Nurs Standard* **9**(49): 52–54

Fruth RM (1991) Differential diagnosis of chest pain. *Crit Care Clin North Am* **3**(1): 59–67

Futterman L, Lemberg L (1997) Endothelium: The key to medical management of coronary artery disease. *Am J Crit Care* **6**(2): 159–167

Fuster V, Badimon L, Badimon J *et al* (1992) The pathogenesis of coronary artery disease and the acute coronary artery syndromes. *New England J Med* **326**(4): 242–249

Garrity TF, Klein RF (1975) Emotional response and clinical severity as early determinants of six month mortality after myocardial infarction. *Heart Lung* **4**(5): 730–737

Gaston-Johansson F, Hofgren C, Watson P *et al* (1991) Myocardial infarction pain: systematic description and analysis. *Intensive Care Nurs* **4**(1): 18–20

Golman L, Cook F, Johnson P *et al* (1996) Prediction of the need for intensive care patients who come to emergency departments with acute chest pain. *N Engl J Med* **334**: 1498–1504

Greenwood D, Packham C, Muir K *et al* (1996) Knowledge of the causes of heart attack among survivors, and implications for health promotion. *Health Educ J* **55**: 215–225

Grines CL (1996) Primary angioplasty — the strategy of choice. *N Engl J Med* **335**(17): 1313–1315

Gruppo Italiano per lo Studio Nell'Infarcto Miocardio, Gissi (1986) The effectiveness of intravenous thrombolytic therapy in caute myocardial infarction. *Lancet* **i**: 397–401

Hamm CW, Ravkilde J, Gerhardt W *et al* (1997) The prognostic value of serum Troponin T in unstable angina. *New Engl J Med* **327**: 146–150

Hannaford P, Kay CR, Ferry S (1994) Agism as explanation for sexism in provision of thrombolysis. *Br Med J* **309**: 573

Hicks S (1994) Standing guard against silent ischaemia and infarction. *Nurs* **24**(1): 34–39

Holdright DR (1996) Chest pain with normal coronary arteries. *Br J Hosp Med* **56**(7): 347–350

Hunink MG, Goldman L, Tosteson A *et al* (1997) The recent decline in mortality from coronary heart disease. *JAMA* **277**: 535–42

Ingham A (1988) The psychological response of patients to admission to coronary care for heart disease, and it's effects on rehabilitation. *Intensive Care Nurs* **4**: 24–33

International Study of Infarct Survival, ISIS-2 (1988) Randomised trial of intravenous streptokinase, oral aspirin, both, or neither among 17 187 cases of suspected acute myocardial infarction. *Lancet* **ii**: 349–360

Jacavone J, Dostal M (1992) A descriptive study of nursing judgement in the assessment and management of cardiac pain. *Adv Nurs Sci* **15**(1): 54–63

Jensen L, King K (1997) Women and heart disease: the issues. *Crit Care Nurse* **17**(2): 45–53

Jowett N, Thompson DR (1995) *Comprehensive coronary care*. Scutari Press, London

Johnson JA, King KB (1995) Influence of expectations about symptoms on delay in seeking treatment during an acute myocardial infarction. *Am J Crit Care* **4**(1): 29–35

Karlik BA, Yarcheski A (1987) Learning needs of the cardiac patient: a partial replication study. *Heart Lung* **16**(5): 544–551

Kernicki J (1993) Differentiating chest pain: Advanced assessment techniques. *Dimen Crit Care Nurs* **12**(2): 66–76

Kleman M, Bickert A, Karpinski A *et al* (1993) Physiologic responses of coronary care patients to visiting. *J Cardiovasc Nurs* **7**(3): 52–62

Kowzlowski-Cepero K (1995) Cocaine-induced myocardial infarction: Treatment with trombolytic therapy. *J Emerg Nurs* **21**(2): 109–111

Lekander B, Lenhmann S, Lindquist R (1993) Therapeutic listening: key intervention for several nursing diagnosis. *Dimensions Crit Care Nurs* **12**(1): 24–29

Lindquist RD (1986) Providing patient opportunities to increase control. *Dimensions Crit Care Nurs* **5**(5): 304–309

Lindsay G, GAW A (1997) *Coronary heart disease prevention: A handbook for the health care team*. Churchill Livingstone, New York: ch 2 and 13

Mackintosh C (1994) Non-reporting of cardiac pain. *Nurs Times* **90**(13): 36–39

Martin GV, Kennedy JW (1994) Choice of thrombolytic agent, In: Julian D, Braunwald E (eds) *Management of acute myocardial infarction*. W B Saunders Company Ltd, London: ch 3

McGovern P, Pankow J, Shahar E *et al* (1996) Recent trends in acute coronary heart disease: Mortality, morbidity, medical care and risk factors. *N Engl J Med* **334**(14): 884–890

Mirka T (1994) Meeting the learning needs of post-myocardial infarction patients. *Nurse Educ Today* **14**: 448–454

Meyer BJ, Chesebro J(1994) Aspirin and anticoagulants. In: Julian D, Braunwald E (eds) *Management of acute myocardial infarction*. WB Saunders Company Ltd, London: Chap 6

Mongiardi F, Payman BC, Hawthorn P (1987) The needs of relatives of patients admitted to the coronary care unit. *Intensive Care Nurs* **3**: 67–70

Murray P (1989) Rehabilitation information and health beliefs in the post-coronary patient: do we meet their information needs? *J Adv Nurs* **14**: 686–693

Neumann F-J, Walter H, Richardt G *et al* (1996) Coronary Palmaz-Schatz stent implantation in acute myocardial infarction. *Heart* **75**: 121–126

Newens AJ, McColl E, Bond S *et al* (1996) Patients' and nurses' knowledge of cardiac-related symptoms and cardiac misconceptions. *Heart Lung* **25**(3): 190–199

Newens AJ, Bond S, Priest JF *et al* (1995) Nurse involvement in cardiac rehabilitation prior to hospital discharge. *J Clin Nurs* **4**: 390–396

Owen A (1995) Tracking the rise and fall of cardiac enzymes. *Nurs 95* **25**(5): 35–38

Pedley H (1996) The nurse's role in pain assessment and management in a coronary care unit. *Intensive Crit Care Nurs* **12**: 254–260

Petrie KJ, Weinman J, Sharpe N *et al* (1996) Role of patients' view of their illness in predicting return to work and functioning after myocardial infarction:longitudinal study. *BMJ* **312**: 1191–1194

Raleigh E, Odtohan C (1987) The effect of a cardiac teaching programme on patient rehabilitation. *Heart Lung* **16**(3): 311–317

Reilly A, Dracup K, Dattolo J (1994) Factors influencing pre-hospital delay in patients experiencing chest pain. *Am J Crit Care* **3**(4): 300–306

Rodriguez A, Fernandez M, Santera O *et al* (1996) Coronary stenting in patients undergoing percutaneous transluminal coronary angioplasty during acute myocardial infarction. *Am J Cardiol* **77**: 685–689

Rowe R (1996) Reasons for pre-hospital delay. *Nurs Times* **92**(8): 40–42

RozenmanY, Gotsman M (1994) The earliest diagnosis of acute myocardial infarction. *Annual Reviews of Medicine* **45**: 31–44

Schneider A (1987) Unreported chest pain. *Focus Crit Care* **14**(5): 21–24

Schwartz LP, Brenner Z (1979) Critical care unit transfer: reducing patient stress through nursing interventions. *Heart Lung* **8**(3): 540–546

Simon S, Phillips K, Badalamenti S *et al* (1997) Current practice regarding visitation policies in critical acer units. *Am J Crit Care* **6**: 210–217

Small SP (1996) Assessment and intervention for ischaemic chest pain: A case study with legal implications for nursing practice. *Prog Cardiovasc Nurs* **11**(3): 17–22

Stewart SL (1992) Acute MI: A review of pathophysiology, treatment and complications. *J Cardiovasc Nurs* **6**(4): 1–25

Sullivan AK, Holdright D, Wright C *et al* (1994) Chest pain in women: clinical, investigative, and prognostic features. *BMJ* **308**: 883–886

Teplitz L, Siwik D (1994) Cellular signals in athero-sclerosis. *J Cardiovasc Nurs* **8**(3): 28–52

Thompson DR, Cordle CJ (1988) Support of wives of myocardial infarction patients. *J Adv Nurs* **13**: 223–228

Thompson DR (1990) *Counselling the coronary care patient and partner*. Scutari Press, London

Thompson DR, Webster R, Sutton T (1994) Coronary care unit patients' and nurses' ratings of intensity of ischaemic chest pain. *Intensive Crit Care Nurs* **10**: 83–88

Thompson DR (1996) The effectiveness of cardiac rehabilitation. *Nurs Crit Care* **1**(5): 214–220

Thompson DR, Bowman GS, Kitson AL *et al* (1996) Cardiac rehabilitation in the United Kingdom: guidelines and audit standards. *Heart* **75**: 89–93

Townsend A (1988) Management of pain in patients with myocardial infarction. *Intensive Care Nurs* **4**(1): 18–20

Wang WT (1994) The educational needs of myocardial infarction patients. *Prog Cardiovasc Nurs* **9**(4): 28–36

Wannamethee G *et al* (1995) Factors determining case fatality in myocardial infarction 'who dies in a heart attack?' *Br Heart J* **74**: 324–331

Weaver WD (1996) The role of thrombolytic drugs in the management of myocardial infarction: Comparative clinical trials. *Euro Heart J* **17**(supplement F): 9–15

Weston C (1993) The pathophysiology of sudden death in athero-sclerotic heart disease. *Resuscitation* **26**: 111–123

Wilhelmsen L (1994) Nitrates. In: Julian D, Braunwald E (eds) *Management of acute myocardial infarction*. W B Saunders Company Ltd, London: ch 9

WilkinsonP, Stevenson R, Randjadayalan K *et al* (1995) Early discharge after myocardial infarction: risks and benefits. *Br Heart J* **74**: 71–75

Wingate S (1990) Post-MI patients' perceptions of their learning needs. *Dimen Crit Care Nurs* **9**(2): 112–118

Yusuf S, Anand A, Avezum A *et al* (1996) Treatment for acute myocardial infarction: Overview of randomised trials. *Euro Heart J* **17** (Supplement F): 16–29

Zerwic JJ, King K, Wlasowicz G (1997) Perceptions of patients with cardiovascular disease about the causes of coronary artery disease. *Heart Lung* **26**(2): 92–98

Ziemann CM, Dracup K (1990) Patient-nurse contracts in critical care: a controlled trial. *Prog Cardiovasc Nurs* **5**(3): 98–103

Index

blood viscosity 108
body mass index 121, 123
body weight 123
brain electrical activity 100
brain herniation 92
brain herniation leading to
  brain stem death 92
brain stem 92
brain stem compression 99
brain tissue 87
bronchial 125
burst suppression 100

C
serious cerebral insult 101
calcium 69, 81
calcium channel blocker 108
calcium channel blockers 154
carbon dioxide elimination 122
cardiac dysrhythmias 12
cardiac enzymes 146
cardiac index 36, 39
cardiac output 35–9, 68
cardiac tamponade 40
cardiogenic shock 48
carina 104
catecholamines 88
catheter
  kinked 51
  infections 52
catheter knotting 44, 54
catheter length 49
causes of acute renal failure
  and identification of
  patient problems 60
causes of coronary artery
  disease 135
central fever 109
central venous pressure 35,
  68
cerebral acidosis 102
cerebral bleed 108
cerebral blood 108
cerebral blood flow 87–8,
  96, 100–1
cerebral blood pressure 97
cerebral blood vessels 102

cerebral blood volume 87,
  102–3, 109
cerebral concussion 89
cerebral contusion 89
cerebral haemodynamics 98,
  100
cerebral hypertension 12,
  110
cerebral hypoxia 99
cerebral impairment 93
cerebral ischaemia 103
cerebral ischemia 102
cerebral metabolic rate 100
cerebral microcirculation 108
cerebral microvasculature 97
cerebral oedema 3, 14, 86–7,
  90, 104–6
cerebral oxygen supply and
  demand parameters 98
cerebral oxygenation 97, 99
cerebral perfusion 108
cerebral perfusion pressure 88,
  95–6
  monitoring 96
cerebral responsiveness to
  carbon dioxide 98
cerebral trauma 90
cerebral vascular bleed 92
cerebral vasculature 87–8, 97
cerebral vasoconstriction 100
cerebral vasodilation 102
cerebro spinal fluid 87
cerebrovascular incident 86
cerebrovascular resistance 87,
  97–8
cerebrovascular spasm 88
cerebrospinal fluid (CSF)
  volume 105
cerebrovascular 104
cerebrovascular haemo-
  dynamics 97
check pH of contents aspirated
  127
chest pain 144–7
classification of renal failure
  60

oxygen extraction 99
oxygen therapy 1, 148–9
oxygen toxicity   14
oxyhaemoglobin   88

P
PA   46
PACs
    manipulation of   41
pain assessment   144–5
PCO_2 102
PCWP   46, 48, 68
PEEP   7, 14, 23, 103
percutaneous tracheostomy 24
percutaneous transluminal coronary angioplasty 152
perforation and balloon rupture   44, 53
perfusion   101
peritoneal   125
pH assessment 126
phlebostatic axis   45
phosphates 24
pituitary   106
planning extubation 22
plaque fracture 138
plaque rupture   138–9
platelet aggregation   139
pneumonia 125
pneumothorax 4, 35
positioning 20
positive end expiratory pressure 8, 12
post diuretic phase   63
post-renal   63
potassium   65, 69, 81
pre-dilution techniques 81
pre-oxygenation   11
preventing complications   163
prevention of complications 148
priorities in a patient requiring haemodynamic monitoring   34

priorities of care for a mechanically ventilated patient   8
    patient with AMI 148
    patient with PAC 43
priorities of care in the patient with acute renal failure requiring haemo-(dia)filtration   66
promoting oxygenation 8
prone position 16
prostaglandins 88
prostoglandin   109
prostoglandin inhibitor 106
protective barrier 118
protein   118
protein mass   121
providing humidification 8
providing physical and emotional support   8
proximal injectate port   37
proximal port   37–8
PTCA 152
pulmonary artery catheter 34–5
pulmonary artery pressure 36, 39
pulmonary aspiration   28
pulmonary capillary perforation 53
pulmonary capillary wedge pressure 36
pulmonary infarction 53
pulmonary oedema   65, 92, 108
pulmonary oxygen toxicity 28
pulmonary secretions   13
pulmonary shunting 5
pulmonary vascular resistance   36, 39
pulsatility index   98
pulse oximetry   7, 19, 22
pupils   95